745.5

745.5   16,195
GRA   Grainger, Sylvia
              Leatherwork

119517

D1605101

LEATHERWORK

Sylvia Grainger

J. B. LIPPINCOTT COMPANY / PHILADELPHIA AND NEW YORK

For help with projects and photography, many thanks to
Linda Bennett, Brian Burns, Joan Conlan, Christy Grainger, Gerry Madden,
Phyllis Perrault, Holly Warner, and Shirley Weiland.

U.S. LIBRARY OF CONGRESS CATALOGING IN PUBLICATION DATA

GRAINGER, SYLVIA, BIRTH DATE
  LEATHERWORK.

  BIBLIOGRAPHY: P.
  SUMMARY: DISCUSSES THE MATERIALS, EQUIPMENT, AND TECHNIQUES OF LEATHER WORK
AND GIVES INSTRUCTION FOR TWENTY-TWO PROJECTS.
    1. LEATHER WORK—JUVENILE LITERATURE. [1. LEATHER WORK. 2. HANDICRAFT] I. TITLE.
TT290.G76   745.53′1   76-21871
ISBN-0-397-31692-5   ISBN-0-397-31693-3 (PBK.)

To Brian

Contents

Before You Begin

First, I want to say that leatherworking is fun! You can make fine things out of leather on your first try, and you do not have to be "artistic" or "good with your hands." All you have to do is read this book carefully, follow the instructions, and go ahead and do it.

To make most of the leatherwork projects in this book, you will follow these steps:

> Cut out the leather pieces
> Bevel the edges
> Punch the holes
> Decorate as desired
> Color the pieces
> Put the project together

These steps are shown and explained in chapters 3, 4, 5, and 6.

Before you start, read the chapters on leather and tools. Then get some scraps of leather and the basic tools listed on pages 18-20. Do a few things to the scraps—cut them, edge them, punch holes in them, lace them together—to get the feel of the tools and leather.

After you've tried out the tools, you'll be ready to start a project. The very simplest projects are first, and you might choose to make one or more of these. After that, you'll find you can make anything you like. Just read the instructions, and remember to try any new process first on scrap.

1.
About Leather

Leather is the hide of an animal (cow, sheep, etc.), changed by chemical processes known as tanning. These processes stop the natural deterioration of the raw hide, making it long-lasting, useful, and beautiful.

Kinds

There are many kinds of leather. In fact, each piece is different, just as each person is different. This is true even though the leather may all have been tanned in the same batch. Since there is so much variation, you need to be able to ask for the right kind for your project. Here are three main types of leather.

OAK-TANNED

Oak-tanned leather is sometimes called "bark-tanned" or "vegetable-tanned." These names mean that the leather is treated with tannic acid, which comes from certain oak trees and other plants. The

main thing to remember about this kind of leather is that it is stiff and can be molded when it is wet. Oak-tanned leather keeps its shape best of all leathers—it flops and stretches least. For this reason, you might want to use oak-tanned cowhide if you are making a project decorated with stamping or carving. When you dampen the leather, the stamps sink right in nicely and make a good, long-lasting decoration.

Here's one way to show yourself how oak-tanned leather works: take a piece of oak-tanned leather, cut it in half, and wet one piece. Now try stamping a design into the dry piece, then the wet piece—you'll notice how much easier it is to stamp into the dampened one. Thin or light-weight oak-tanned cowhide makes good wallets, since it can be very thin and still hold its shape.

When you're looking at leather in a supply store, look for light brown, slightly pinkish leather. Keep in mind that you can dye the leather any color. See if it feels somewhat stiff—if so, you probably have oak-tanned. Now smell the leather. Oak-tanned has a special smell—a good one! Keep sniffing around, and soon you will be able to tell a piece of oak-tanned cowhide just by the smell. One last thing: oak-tanned leather usually squeaks when it is rolled up. Other kinds of leather don't usually do that. Roll up a piece of suede and listen—no squeak there.

CHROME-TANNED

Chrome-tanned leather has been tanned with chromium salts. It is the opposite of oak-tanned, in a way—chrome-tanned leather is soft,

floppy, and pliable. Vests and other clothes can be made out of chrome-tanned cowhide and sheepskin. You can imagine what a vest made out of oak-tanned would be like—stiff, uncomfortable, and ridiculous-looking. You might also use chrome-tanned leather for a soft pouch, a cap, moccasins, pillows.

This kind of leather can be made with a fuzzy nap on one side, and then it is called suede (pronounced SWAYED). Sometimes the tannery will make both sides usable—one smooth and one sueded. Chrome-tanned leather is often called "garment" leather. It comes dyed in many, many colors, and you should pick the one you want, since it's not a good idea to dye garment leather yourself (it's hard to get the color even).

Here are some kinds of chrome-tanned leather you may find:

Garment cowhide: Sometimes the suede side only is good, sometimes the smooth side only, sometimes both are usable. This is made in many thicknesses and colors. Sometimes it is thin enough to be sewn on a home sewing machine.

Sheepskin suede: Really fine-grained suede; small skins.

Split cowhide suede: This is always sueded on both sides. It is what's left over on the underside when a cowhide is split to the thickness the tannery wants, so it has no top or smooth grain. This suede is all right to use as long as there will not be any strain on it—it is weak and will split if it is used for pants, jackets, etc. This is especially true when the split cowhide is very thin.

Sheep shearling: With the wool left on one side and suede on the other side. You can make beautiful hats, slippers, and vests with sheep shearling. It's also nice just to have a shearling around! It's called "shearling" because the wool side has been sheared, or trimmed, to an even thickness, usually about ⅜ to ½ inch. Mostly, shearling has a brown or gold suede side and a white or off-white nap (wool) side, but occasionally you will find some with dark suede and dark fur. (It's been dyed that way—it doesn't come from a black sheep.)

Deerskin: Deerskin is extremely soft; the skins are small, usually ragged and full of holes and scratches, and very expensive. The color is almost always gold.

Buck-tanned cowhide: This cowhide has been specially treated to feel like buck, or deerskin. It's really soft and spongy and feels somewhat stretchy. Buck-tanned cowhide is usually suede on the inside, and it makes really nice pouches, vests, soft bags, and moccasins. Quite often you'll see it dyed a gold color, like deerskin, but it can be dyed any color at the tannery.

RETANNED

Leather that has been both oak-tanned *and* chrome-tanned is called retanned, because it is tanned twice. It is somewhat softer than oak-tanned leather, and somewhat stiffer than chrome-tanned. Besides using both types of chemicals, the tannery usually soaks the hides for a while in hot oil and wax; this is called stuffing. A retanned hide has a slightly waxy, oily feel. Each tannery does it a bit differently.

You will be working with one kind of retanned cowhide a lot—it's called latigo (pronounced LAT-a-go). Latigo is a favorite of many craftspeople, and when you begin working with it, you'll know why. It makes fine purses, belts, wristbands, key rings—just about anything except clothes. Latigo is most often dyed yellow at the tannery, and when you put a finish on it, the natural grain and markings on the hide show through, making a really fine, interesting effect.

There are many other kinds of retanned leather, and you'll begin to recognize them with practice.

Shape, Size, and Thickness

When you buy sheepskin, you will probably get the whole hide. When you buy cowhide, however, it will almost certainly be cut in half, and it will be called a side. (Tannery machines aren't big enough to process a whole cowhide at once.) Here is a side of cowhide, marked to show the belly (most stretchy part) and the backbone (least stretchy part). The small hide on top is a sheepskin.

Another shape you might find is called a double shoulder. This cut has a lot of waste trimmed away, and is most often found in oak-tanned, for making belts.

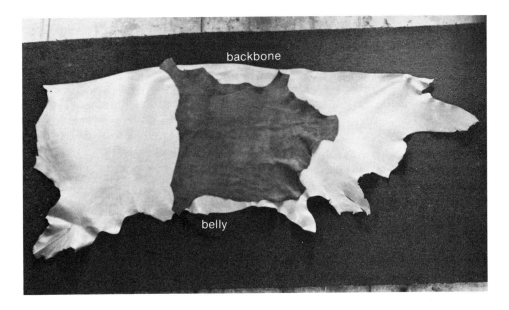

Leather is measured at the tannery, in square feet. Look for the mark on the back side of the piece. It will say the number of square feet and quarters of a square foot. For example, 20-1 means twenty and one-quarter square feet (20¼), 10-2 means ten and two-quarters square feet (10²/₄), 6-3 means six and three-quarters square feet (6¾). A side of cowhide is about twenty square feet, a double shoulder of cowhide is about ten square feet, and a sheepskin is about seven square feet.

Hides are split into different thicknesses while they are being tanned, so they can be used for different purposes. Leather thickness is measured in a strange way—in ounces. This used to mean the number of ounces one square foot weighed. For example, one square foot of "eight-ounce" leather would weigh about eight ounces on the scale. Here's the way it's done now:

one-ounce leather = $1/64''$ thick   ——————

two-ounce leather = $2/64$ or $1/32''$ thick ——————

four-ounce leather = $4/64$ or $1/16''$ thick ■■■■■

six-ounce leather = $6/64$ or $3/32''$ thick ■■■■■

eight-ounce leather = $8/64$ or $1/8''$ thick ■■■■■

As you can see, the more "ounces," the thicker the piece of leather.

Here's a rough idea of the uses of different thicknesses. Remember that a piece of leather can be stiff but thin, or it can be soft but thick, depending on how it was tanned (oak-tanned, chrome-tanned, or re-tanned) as well as on how thick or thin it was split at the tannery.

About two-ounce: Wallet linings, clothes, soft bags, pillow covers, moccasins.

About four-ounce: Wallets, moccasins, watchbands, notebooks.

About six-ounce: Purses, wristbands, boxes, sandal straps, notebooks.

About eight-ounce: Belts, sandal top soles.

After you have been working with leather for a while, you'll be able to tell the weight just by feeling it.

Quality

Grading (separating according to quality) is done in different ways at different tanneries. Sometimes a tannery separates the hides into grades 1 (the best), 2, 3, and so on; sometimes into grades A, B, C, etc. TR means "tannery run." Tannery run hides are *not* separated according to how good they are. Usually, the grade is not marked on a tannery run hide at all.

Even the top grades will have "imperfections," since leather is a natural material. There will be some holes, scratches, grain markings, wrinkles, brands (see the picture)—and you can often use these as part of the design of your project. The main way you will be able to tell good leather from not-so-good leather is by your experience. Take time to look around a bit; ask if you can see different grades and different kinds of leather. A really fine piece of leather has few or no brands or holes in it, few cuts on the back side, and a nice-looking grain (smooth)

side. It shouldn't be really shiny and painted-looking, because then you can't see the grain, and it probably couldn't be dyed at all.

Buying Leather

Pieces of leather are sold by the square foot. For example, the price for a side of cowhide might be $1.75 per square foot. A side is usually about twenty square feet, so the price for the side would be around $35.00 (20 × $1.75). The price varies a lot, depending on the type and grade of leather and which tannery it came from. In general, you will find prices ranging from about $1.00 per square foot for low-grade split cowhide all the way up to about $2.40 per square foot for oak-tanned cowhide of the best grade with the waste removed. It's usually worth the extra money to get the best you can—you will have less throwaway scrap, and you will have a much nicer project.

Will you have to buy a whole side? Each supplier is different. Ask questions: Do you sell only whole pieces, or will you cut off a piece? Do you have scraps? Some places sell only full sides; some sell punched-out kits in boxes; some have straps, belts, and laces cut; some will cut a piece off a side for you. If possible, keep looking until you find a place where the people who wait on you know how to work with leather themselves (you'll be able to tell!) and are happy to talk to you and help you get the right things. If you have a pattern, take it with you when you go to buy, so that you can make sure it fits on the leather.

Perhaps you'll be buying your supplies by mail order—go ahead and ask any questions you have by letter. There is a list of stores that sell leather, tools, and other supplies—with notes about the way they sell—at the back of this book. Also, you can look in the Yellow Pages of the phone book, under Leather. Most often, stores that sell leather also sell leatherworking tools and other supplies.

With a bit of looking around, you may be able to find free scraps. Remember that the company or leatherworkers would probably use the leather themselves if it was in big, first-rate pieces—but sometimes you can get scraps worth practicing on or even using for projects. Ask a leather shop, a sandalmaker, a crafts teacher, a shoe repair shop, a tannery, a leather supply store, perhaps a leather goods factory.

Lacing

For many of your projects, you'll need to buy lacing, thin strips of leather used to lace or sew pieces of a project together. Most leather supply stores sell lacing by the yard or by the foot. The price is usually from about 7 cents to 15 cents per foot. Sometimes lacing comes cut to a certain length—often 6 or 7 feet—and sometimes you can ask for the exact length you want.

Here are some kinds you'll be looking for:

Latigo or oak-tanned lacing (a), to match the leather you're using (for purse, belt pouch, etc.). This lacing should be 3/16 inch wide, which is a little bigger than the hole it will go into. The lacing will stretch out a bit as you pull it through the holes, and the lacing should end up snug in the holes, for looks and strength.

With a little practice, you can cut your own latigo or oak-tanned lacing, using The Strap Cutter. If possible, cut the lacing straight down the backbone edge of the side, since that's the least stretchy place.

Chrome-tanned (soft) lacing (b) is used for the pouch, the shearling hat, perhaps for the knapsack. It can be used to lace up clothes— —anything made of soft leather or suede. It should be ¼ inch wide— —even wider in relation to the hole it goes through than the latigo lacing—because it is softer and thinner and will stretch out somewhat more. Try cutting your own soft lacing, either with The Strap Cutter or with shears. Slight irregularities won't matter, you'll find, as the lacing will straighten out when it is pulled through the holes. Often, you won't be able to buy lacing to match the soft leather you want—a good reason to try cutting your own.

Calf or goat lacing (c) is thin and narrow (⅛ inch wide). It is used in #0

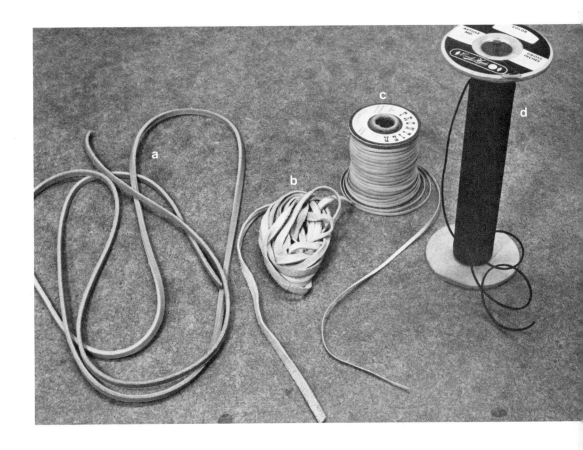

(^{1}/$_{16}$") holes. This lacing usually comes in 50-yard spools; you may have to buy the whole spool. Use calf or goat lacing for the visor and notebook cover; it is also used for wallets and fancy lacing projects. These laces come in many colors; you can either dye your own or choose the color you want. Lacing made from calfskin is not much different from that made from goatskin; goatskin has a more grainy look and is said to be a little stronger, but the difference is not enough to worry about—just choose whichever looks best to you.

Cordohyde (d) is the brand name of a small round cotton cord which looks like leather. It is very useful for hanging pendants, mirrors, wall hangings, and the like.

2.

About Tools

There are some tools you will need for sure, and some you can choose from, depending on what you want to make. Under Basic Tools, you'll find the tools you definitely need for most projects. To find out what *other* tools you need for a particular project, check the tool list for that project. For example, if you want to make wristbands with snaps, you'll need a snap setter in addition to the basic tools. Decorating tools aren't in the "must-have" section; you can make many things without them—but you'll probably want to get at least one.

Look for leatherworking tools at a store which specializes in leather supplies (under Leather in the Yellow Pages).

Basic Tools

First, the tools you must have, in the order you'll use them.

LEATHERWORKERS' GOLDEN RULE: TRY IT FIRST ON SCRAP!

Pencil (a), for drawing the pattern onto the leather. It's important to use a soft pencil, not a hard pencil or pen, so you can erase if you make a mistake.

Cutter, to cut the pieces out. You can use a razor cutter (b)—a single-edged razor blade in a holder—or a pair of leather shears (c). Razor blades are thinner than other types of blades, so they cut more easily. Razor cutters are very inexpensive (under $1.00), and they work fine.

Leather shears are terrific, but they are *expensive.* A pair will cost around $7.50 to $15.00, and the higher-priced ones are usually better.

16

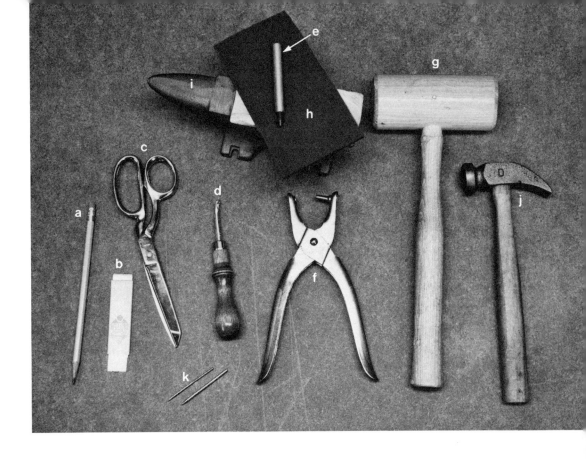

If you can, get a good pair. Try them out before you buy them. They should have serrated blades (very small bumps on the cutting edges).

Edger (d). This rounds the edge of the leather so that it wears evenly and is more comfortable where it touches you, as on wristbands and visors. Also, when you dye an edged piece, the edge will have a nice dark outline. I use an edger on both the front and back of nearly everything I make, except when I am using very thin or soft leather. Edgers come in sizes 0, 1, 2, 3, 4, and 5—the bigger the number, the more the edger cuts off. Get yourself a #2 edger; it's a good size for nearly everything. Edgers cost around $2.00. (They are also called edge bevelers.)

Punch, for making holes for things like rivets, lacing, sewing, and snaps. You can use a drive punch (e) or a spring punch (f).

A drive punch usually costs less than a spring punch (about $1.50 for a drive punch, $3.00 for a spring punch). It's called a drive punch because you "drive" it with a mallet through the leather into a piece of wood or thick rubber. To start, you really only need one size—a #5, which makes a 5/32″ hole.

The spring punch is faster to use than the drive punch. Again, you need only the #5-size punch to start. Please don't get a rotary-type

17

punch, with all different sizes on a wheel, even though it looks like such a good deal. Almost always, this type of punch wears out, and the wheel slips after a while; also, the different size punches chew up the small copper anvil they punch onto—so the punch doesn't cut cleanly. Anyway, you only need one or possibly two sizes of holes.

Some leatherworkers like to have both drive and spring punches, because the spring punch is more convenient to use, but the drive punch will punch holes where the spring punch can't reach, away from the edge of the leather.

Mallet (g), for pounding your drive punch and decorating stamps. Get a wooden, rawhide, or rubber mallet. It's easier to pound those tools with a mallet than with a metal hammer, and they will last longer. If possible, try out the mallet for size before buying it. The size and weight are not of critical importance, but a tiny toy mallet won't do the job well, and a great heavy one will tire your arm unnecessarily.

Rubber soling material (h), to go on top of the anvil when drive punches or slot punches are used. Get a piece at least 3 by 5 inches, about ¼ inch thick. You can buy this where you get the other tools, or at a shoe repair shop. It is possible to use a piece of wood underneath the drive punches and slot punches instead of the rubber and anvil, and many people do it that way, but I find the rubber and anvil way to be the easiest and safest.

Anvil (i), for setting rivets and snaps and for stamping. The anvil also goes under the piece of rubber soling material for the drive punch. You can use any heavy, flat metal thing—a piece of scrap iron, a bench vise, the side of a large hammer, the back of a cast iron frying pan——anything, as long as it is heavy, flat metal and won't be damaged by being pounded on.

Hammer (j). A metal hammer is used for setting rivets, setting snaps, and tapping lacing flat. It doesn't have to be a special type of hammer, although one with a slightly rounded head is easiest to use for rivets.

Lacing needle (k). This tool makes lacing easy. There are several kinds; the best kind is a brass tube with screw threads in one end, so you can screw the lacing needle onto the lacing. You will probably want two sizes: one for the heavier latigo lacing (purses, etc.) and one for the smaller, lightweight calf lacing (visor, etc.).

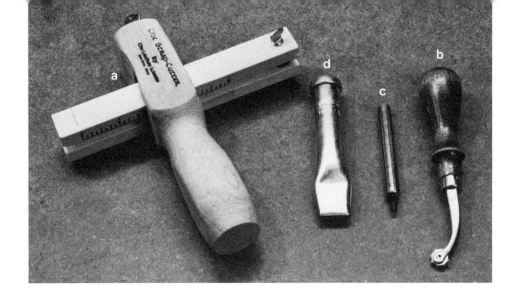

Tools You May Want

The Strap Cutter (a). You can cut even, accurate straps, belts, and laces with this patented tool. It uses a razor blade to cut—hidden in the two crossbars, so you cannot cut yourself. Don't buy the kind with the blade sticking up out of one crossbar; it is cheaper but dangerous, and harder to use. You can save quite a bit on leather by cutting up your own leather into strips. The Strap Cutter costs around $8.50; you can usually save this amount the first few times you use the tool.

Stitchmarker (b). The stitchmarker marks stitches! As you push the wheel across the leather, points on the wheel mark a row of evenly spaced dots. Evenly spaced stitches can be marked with a pencil and ruler, or even with a kitchen fork—but if you do a lot of sewing or lacing where you punch small holes, you might want this tool. Stitch-markers come in different sizes; I recommend the one which marks five stitches to the inch.

Smaller size punch. If you decide to make things which are sewn (like the coin purse), or laced with small lacing (like the visor), you need one more punch—a #0 size punch, for $1/16''$ holes. You can get either a drive punch (c) or a spring punch, but remember that sewing and small lacing often mean lots of holes, so you might want to choose the more convenient spring punch.

Slot punch (d). This is a special kind of drive punch which makes slots for buckle tongues, decorations, and so on. If you need to make a slot and you don't have one of these, you can punch two round holes, one at either end of the slot you want to make, and connect these holes with the razor cutter. Or you can nibble along with the #5 round punch until you have a slot. Slot punches come in many sizes; the one that makes a hole ⅝ inch long is a good choice. You can move the punch over and punch again to make a longer slot, if necessary. Slot punches cost about $3.00 to $4.00 and are also called bag punches.

Stamps (e), for imprinting designs in the leather. The average price of a stamp is around $2.50. There are hundreds of stamps to choose from. Unless you see a design you really like right away, you might have trouble deciding which one to get. I suggest that for your first stamp, you choose one that doesn't make a picture all by itself (horse, rose, fish, etc.) but will make lots of different designs when used in different ways. *Two* stamps like that, used together, really increase the possibilities. Of course, if you see a picture stamp which hollers "Take me home!" then by all means, you should take that one home.

Marble (f). You can stamp onto your anvil, but it is really nice to have a thick piece of marble for this job, especially if you do a lot of stamping. If you put wet leather onto the anvil it may rust after a while, and the low, flat, larger surface of the marble is more convenient.

Dividers or compass (g). A really useful tool for making guidelines and planning decorations. Look for it in an art supply store, a stationery store, or a dime store.

Swivel knife (h), for drawing designs in the leather. The part below the stirrup-shaped finger rest swivels, making it possible to cut curved lines easily. A swivel knife costs around $2.50.

Modeling tool (i). A modeling tool can be used to smooth out and deepen swivel knife cuts. Some craftspeople like to use the modeling tool instead of a pencil to make light guidelines and to trace designs.

V-gouge (j). The adjustable V-gouge makes a V-shaped cut in the leather. It was designed to make a cut on the back side of a piece of leather, to make it fold easily—but the V-gouge makes a fine decorating tool also. It removes a small strip of leather instead of just slicing through the grain of the leather as a swivel knife does, so the resulting line is wider.

Edge creaser (k). This is a decorating tool; it makes a borderline along the edge of a piece of leather. There are different sizes; try them out if you can—a #3 is a good size.

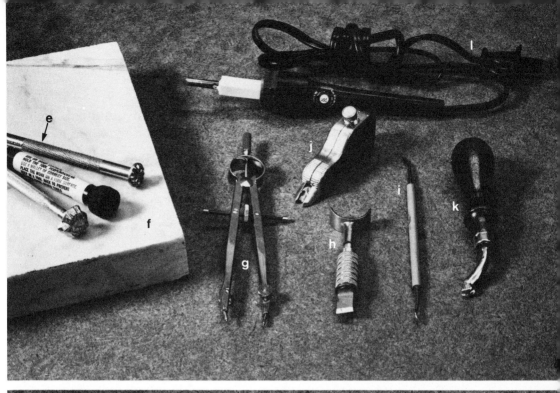

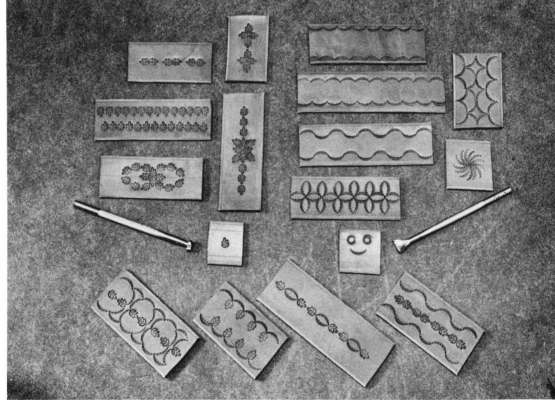

Woodburning tool (l). An electric pen, or woodburning tool, the kind that gets hot when you plug it in, makes a good decorating tool.

Paintbrush (m), for applying dye or paint to small areas. It's best to have a good quality one; cheap ones tend to fall apart, and they make it harder to paint tiny areas. If your leather supply store doesn't have brushes, buy one in an art supply store. Size #3 is a good one for most work; for very fine lines and tiny areas you might want to get a smaller one, perhaps #0 or #00.

Snap setter and snaps. The best kind of snap setter has three parts: a small cupped anvil (n), which goes under the rounded snap cap; a holder (o), which holds the snap parts in place; and a pin (arrow), which fits inside the holder and is pounded with the hammer to set the snap. There are two sizes of snap setter. One is for the Durable Dot snap, used for heavy leather (eight-ounce and over); the other is smaller, for the Baby Durable Dot snap, used for thinner leather (seven-ounce and under). Snap setters usually cost around $3.50. Solid brass Dot brand snaps (the best kind) are around 10 cents each; there are four parts to each snap.

#000 glovers' needle (p) is a sharp needle with a three-sided point. It is used for sewing soft leather or suede by hand, with waxed thread. #000 is the biggest size made and is by far the easiest to use.

#000 harness needles (q) are dull-pointed needles. They are used for

hand stitching, with waxed thread, when there are holes already punched in the leather. Often, you will need two needles at once for the seam. They are not expensive (about 10 cents each), so get at least two.

Shoe brush (r), a great help for buffing the finished product to a lovely gloss. A soft rag will also do it.

Other supplies. Many of the projects call for specific types of hardware (rivets or Chicago posts for fastening; shoe tacks; D-ring and leash clip for dog leash; buckle for belt, etc.). These are listed with the materials at the beginning of the directions for each project. Products for coloring and finishing leather are discussed in the chapter on Coloring Leather; choose and buy the color(s) you want after you've chosen the leather for a project.

Other Things to Collect for Your Workplace

You need a *table* to work on—something sturdy that doesn't bounce around a lot when you pound. It's a good idea to put a piece of *plywood or Masonite* on the top of the table or bench, so you can cut and hammer away without worrying about the surface of the table.

Get together a stack of *newspapers,* for spreading on the table when you are going to use dyes and finishes.

Regular kitchen *paper towels* are best for wiping off Acrylic Antique Finish. You can also use soft rags.

Your tools will love you if you put them in a good *storage place.* A box is all right to start with, but tools do tend to hit against each other and may get dulled. The best thing is to hang them up. Then they are always where you can find them, and they can't get damaged. A tool board is handy for this purpose; directions for making one are on page 77.

If you plan to make any patterns of your own, equip your workshop with a supply of *plain paper*—large pieces, and heavy if possible. Paper with squares marked on it is nice to work with.

Add a *ruler or yardstick* for measuring and drawing straight lines. A *square or T-square* comes in handy, too, for drawing square corners.

You'll need *wax* for waxing lacing. You can buy paraffin blocks very cheaply in a grocery store or craft store; you can also use a candle end or a piece of beeswax.

How Much Does It Cost to Get Started?

You can get a razor cutter, edger, #5 drive punch, lacing needle, and a piece of rubber soling material for around $6.00. If you can find a mallet, hammer, anvil, and pencil at home, you're all set to get started! If you don't have those, figure on spending somewhere around $16.00 all together. After that, you can choose—perhaps you want to add a stamp or two, or maybe shears are what you really would like to have next. Remember to check the tool list for each project you want to make, to see if you need special tools.

You can save money and perhaps have a better set of tools to use if you can get together with other leatherworkers. For example, you might buy a side of leather and cut it up, rather than getting small pieces. In some cases, quantity discounts are available; many stores give a 10 percent discount when you buy three or more stamps at a time, for instance. You might also buy equipment as a group and work together.

3.
Cutting, Beveling, and Punching

The first step in making most leatherwork projects is to prepare the pattern and draw it onto the top (smooth) side of the leather.

To use the patterns in this book, trace them onto a sheet of paper, and cut out the traced pattern pieces. Tape pieces together along the dotted lines, if necessary.

Now, transfer the pattern to the leather. It's important to draw on the top side, because it's easier to cut and punch with the top side up. Hold the pattern in place with your hand if it is a small pattern; if it's too large to hold down securely with one hand, weight the pattern down with heavy things like an anvil, books, or shears. Draw around the pattern with a soft lead pencil. Draw in holes and other markings, too, by pressing on the paper with the pencil. This will mark the leather even though the pencil doesn't actually touch the leather. Designs can be marked this way too, right through the paper.

Note that some patterns (knapsack, hatchet cover, shoulder strap bag, chessboard) are just guides for making your own full-sized pattern, so you won't be tracing these.

Cutting

If you are using a razor cutter rather than leather shears, put your leather on a large piece of wood or Masonite, so you don't damage your table or bench. Here's a trick for easy and accurate cutting with a razor cutter: put your finger down on the very end of the top side of the cutter, as the picture shows. All at once, sink the blade into the leather. Now, with your other hand, pull the leather. Don't move the cutter. If you pull the leather and keep the cutter still, the cutter won't wobble around, and you can't cut yourself. In any case, keep the fingers of the hand that is holding the leather in front of the cutter, never behind it—to make sure you don't cut your fingers.

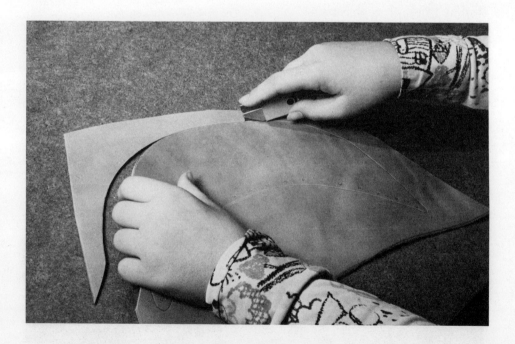

When the blade gets chipped or dulled, just pull the case of the cutter off and change the blade. It's a good idea to change the blade often, since it's much easier to cut with a fresh blade. The blades are not expensive.

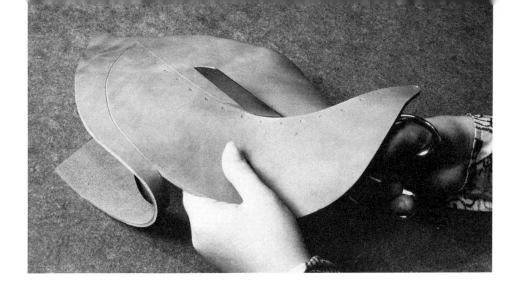

Use leather shears the same way as ordinary scissors. Be especially careful with them so as not to cut yourself. They are very sharp!

You may want to use The Strap Cutter to cut out parts of the project—a strap or belt or perhaps your own lacing. If you are starting with a full side of leather, cut these along the backbone edge of the side (the straightest edge), since the backbone is the least stretchy part of the side. You'll need to make a straight edge to start from, so put the side on a large table or on the floor. Lay it out flat, smooth top-grain side up. Draw a straight pencil line all the way down the backbone edge of the side, using a yardstick. Cut along this pencil line with your shears or razor cutter. Adjust The Strap Cutter to the width you want, and start the cut, holding The Strap Cutter by the handle (not by the crossbars). As soon as the end of the strap comes through, take hold of the end and pull on it. Don't shove the leather through or pull on the main piece of leather—just pull on the strap you are cutting off. This is important for a straight cut.

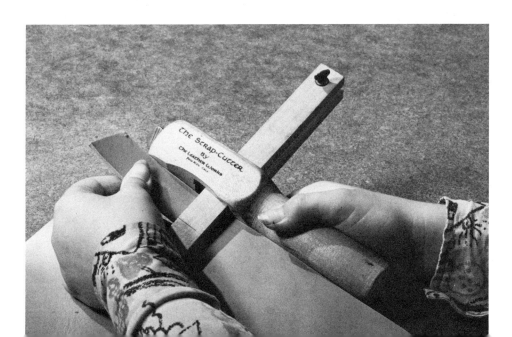

Beveling

To bevel an edge, press down on the edger and slide it along the edge, holding it at an angle. When you try this on a scrap of leather, experiment with the way you hold the edger to get the best angle—try it with your edger held up higher, down lower, leaning to the right or to the left.

As you bevel, move your other hand along, keeping it very near to where you are edging; you'll find it a lot easier that way, because your other hand can hold the leather firmly in place. Don't worry, you cannot hurt yourself with an edger. And you can't cut off too much. It's a little harder to edge the back side of the leather than the front—you may need to move the edger back and forth a bit instead of just sliding it along.

To sharpen an edger, wrap a piece of very fine sandpaper (500 or 600 grit) around a ruler, and rub the edger back and forth on the edge. You might want to sharpen your new edger before using it, since sometimes edgers are dull when you get them.

Punching

First, mark the holes. The placement of the holes may be marked on the pattern, and then you'll be marking them on the leather at the same time you draw the pattern. For sewing, and sometimes for small lacing, you can use the stitchmarker to mark the placement of the holes. Until you have had some practice with the stitchmarker, you may want to make a very light guideline with a pencil, to show where the stitchmarker should go. Press the stitchmarker pretty hard for good marks;

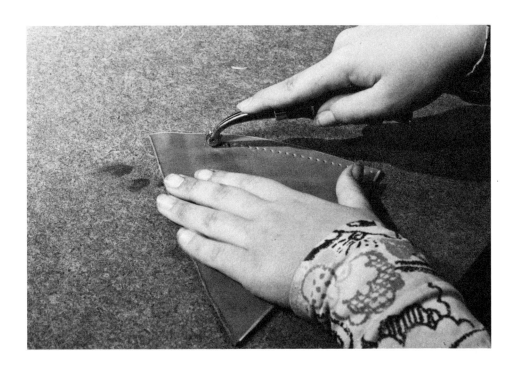

sometimes it helps to run the marker back and forth over a short space in the same marks until they are easy to see.

To punch holes with the drive punch, set your anvil in a secure place on the table. A good place is over the table leg, so the anvil won't bounce around. If your table is wobbly, you might want to put the anvil on the floor. Then put the rubber soling material on the anvil to protect the cutting edge of the punch. *Never* pound your drive punch through the leather into anything made of metal, concrete, or cement—if you do, you will smash the cutting edge of the punch flat and it won't cut anymore.

Put the leather on the rubber, the drive punch on the leather, and pound the punch with the mallet. At first, it will take quite a bit of pounding, but after you've done it several times, you'll find that it only takes a couple of whacks. The punch has a place for the little "holes" to come out—either at the top or the side—and you do not have to pick the leather piece out of the end of the punch each time you punch a hole.

Use slot punches the same way as drive punches. If you have trouble

getting a slot punch to cut, first look at the cutting edge to see if it has been dulled by pounding against metal. Then, if the edge is sharp, try tipping the punch to one end of the slot and then the other, giving it a couple of whacks each time. Finally, hold it straight and finish off the slot. (If the cutting edge *has* been pounded against metal, the unfortunate truth is that you'll have to get another punch.)

When you use your spring punch, hold the handle as close to the end as you can—you get more power, or leverage, that way. A new punch

may be stiff until you've punched a couple of holes. If you have trouble, here are some things to try. Twist the punch as you squeeze it; try to squeeze all at once instead of slowly; and try putting the handle of the punch on the table and pressing with both hands.

Your punches—drive, spring or slot—should last a long, long time if you protect them from dropping against metal surfaces. They do not need sharpening. One good way to keep a spring punch cutting well is to put a rubber band around the handle to keep it closed when you are not using it. Then the punch tube can never get chipped.

4.
Decorating Your Project

Any project made of oak-tanned or retanned leather can be decorated with cut and/or stamped designs. There is one rule for decorating leather: Do it exactly the way you like it! (Or leave it plain; leather often has grain and other markings which are interesting and beautiful as they are.) The only way to learn is to try something and see how it turns out, then improve it (or do it the same) the next time. So I will not give you any more rules—only some ideas, suggestions, and starting places.

Whenever you cut or stamp oak-tanned leather, dampen it first. I just run the leather under the faucet, once on the top side and once on the back; shake off the extra water; and wait a minute or two for the water to sink in. You might keep a wet sponge handy in case the leather gets too dry as you go. After a little practice, you will know exactly how damp the leather should be—not soggy wet, but evenly damp, something like clay. When the leather dries out, it will become firm again and hold the design you have cut or stamped into it. If you are using latigo or another retanned leather, you do not need to dampen it.

Cutting Designs

You can "draw" on leather with a swivel knife, V-gouge, or electric pen. The best designs for this purpose are simple line drawings, without too many tiny lines or details. You can draw directly on the leather with a pencil before cutting, but it's a good idea to plan your design on paper first. You can draw a picture. Or you can make a design with lines which divide up the space. They could be straight lines, or curved lines, or both.

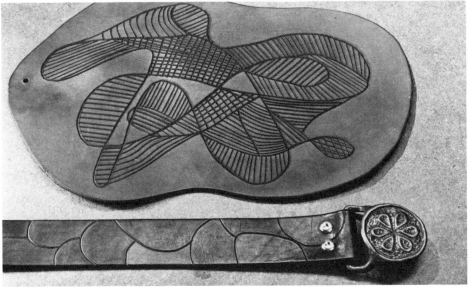

A "mandala" or snowflake-type design is good for any piece where
you have some space—a wall hanging, a purse flap, a notebook cover.
Use a square piece of paper (a little smaller than the leather) which is
somewhat stiff, but which you can see through at least a little. Fold it
the way you do to make "snowflakes"—in half, in half again, and then
diagonally in half again. Draw a simple design on the folded piece with
a heavy black felt marker. Refold the piece so you can see the design

33

on another part of the paper, and trace it. Do that again and again until you have traced a whole design.

Other fine design ideas are just waiting to pour out of your imagination onto your project (don't spill any!) and they are also all around you. Here are some places to look for designs. In some cases, you'll want to use the whole design just as it is, and sometimes you'll want to take just a part of the design, leaving out things that make it too complicated. And sometimes what you find will just be the beginning for a design of your own. Look for designs in stores, on package labels, on boxes; on greeting cards; in books—if you like birds, for example, look in a library book about birds; in coloring books—there are lots of good ones now, on shells, butterflies, antique cars, and so on; outside—look around at buildings, trees, flowers, leaves; on cloth—printed fabrics often have good design ideas; in paperbacks published by Dover, which have designs of all sorts—a few of the best ones for leather are listed in the bibliography at the end of this book.

What should you do with the design when you find it? Somehow you need to get it onto a piece of paper which is just the right size and shape for your leather project. Depending on where the design is, you can draw around it, or trace it, or look at it and draw it yourself. Remember to keep it simple. If the design you want is too small and you can't draw it bigger, trace it onto paper that has small squares on it. Then make bigger squares on another piece of paper and draw the design by comparing where the lines go on the squares. You can make a big design smaller by going from big squares to smaller ones.

When you have the design on paper, put it on the undyed leather and hold it in place with heavy objects. Then use a pencil to draw over the design. The leather underneath will mark easily when you press on the paper with the pencil. Carefully look to make sure the design is all there on the leather before you move the paper. Once the design has been transferred to the leather, you can choose among several tools to cut along the lines.

Swivel knife. With a swivel knife, you can draw around curves. To use the swivel knife, put the end of your index finger on the "stirrup" finger rest. Hold the middle part with your thumb and third or fourth finger, and rest your little finger on the leather. Tip the *top* end of the knife *away* from you and pull the knife *toward* you. Press fairly hard to make a deep cut. Practice making a few straight cuts first, then try some curves and wavy lines. Notice that you can swivel the blade to make

34

curves without turning your index finger or your arm. When you're cutting a tight curve, try turning the leather slowly as you cut; sometimes it's easier that way.

Modeling tool. To smooth and deepen a swivel knife cut, run a modeling tool along the cut.

V-gouge. The V-gouge makes a V-shaped cut. To use it, turn the screw on the top to make the blade come out the bottom until it cuts as deeply as you want. When you are cutting, keep the V-gouge flat (don't tip it) and slide it along, so that the cut will be even. Set your V-gouge on its side when not in use, so the blade won't get chipped.

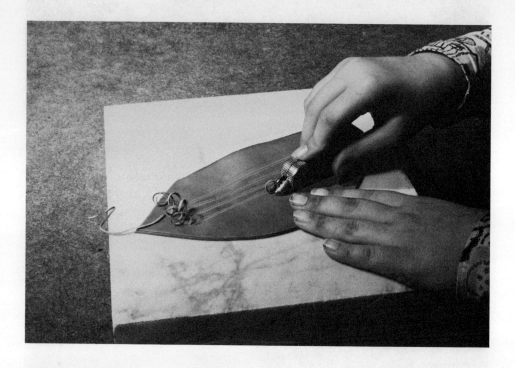

Edge creaser. This tool makes a borderline around a piece of leather. To use it, press it along the edge of your project. The line will show up more when you put on Acrylic Antique Finish.

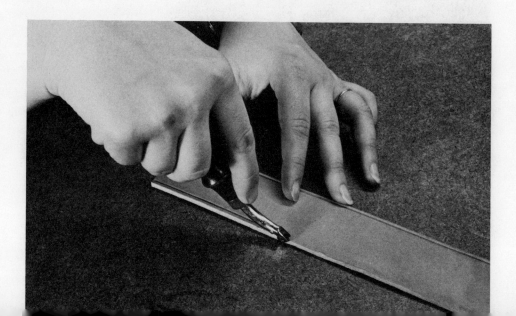

Woodburning tool or electric pen. Try the electric pen out on a few scraps of the kind of leather you're using, since it looks different on each type of leather. It will work especially well on most chrome-tanned leather (the soft kind). Of course, you have to make sure that you don't leave the hot tip in one place on the leather too long, or it will burn a hole. With a little practice, you can write with the electric pen.

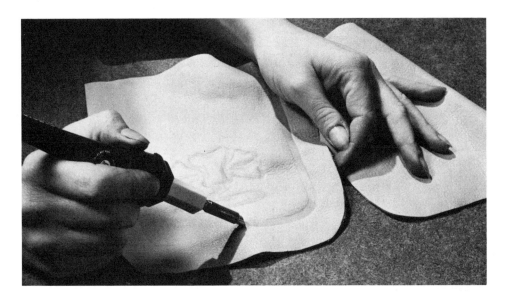

Stamping

Stamps are great fun and easy to use. They can be used alone or combined with swivel knife or other cut lines. Do all stamping before using dyes and finishes so the color can sink into the deep places.

Different types of leather stamp differently. Oak-tanned takes stamps the best; remember to dampen both sides before stamping. Latigo (retanned) stamps fine, too, but you don't need to dampen it first. Chrome-tanned leather does not stamp well.

To use stamps, put your leather on either your anvil or a piece of marble. Don't stamp onto wood or concrete. You need a very dense backing material for the leather, so that it cannot move out of the way of the stamp, or bounce around. This way the stamp will make a single good impression. Spread your fingers out on the stamp, to hold it steady; try putting your little finger on the bottom of the stamp or on the leather. Now hit the stamp with a mallet, not a metal hammer. If the stamp doesn't go deep enough, you can put it back, carefully, and wiggle it a bit to make sure it's in the same place. Then give it a few more whacks with the mallet. Make sure you stamp deeply, so the design will last.

Alphabet and number sets. These sets come with a single handle that fits all the stamps. To use these, put the handle in the letter or number you want. There is a tiny guide letter or number on the stamp. Place this toward you, and the stamp will turn out right side up. If you stamp a letter upside down or in the wrong place, sometimes it works to stamp the right letter on top of the wrong one. Stamp it in deep, and it may cover up the mistake.

Here's a tip for spacing words, names, etc.: Measure to the middle of the place where you want the word or words. Figure out which is the middle letter, and stamp it in the middle place. Then you can put in the rest of the letters, working out from the middle.

Shaders (a). Shaders are pear-shaped stamps which press down an area smoothly to create a three-dimensional effect. They are usually used inside a space outlined by a swivel knife line, like the flower petals in the photo. To use a shader, tap the stamp lightly with the mallet, and move the tool slightly each time you tap. If you have only one shader, and it's too big for the area you want to shade, tip the stamp so that you're only using a part of it. After you have dyed a piece done this

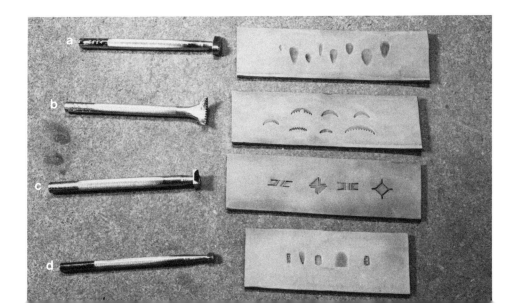

way, you'll see why this stamp is called a shader; the Acrylic Antique Finish makes the shaded area come out darker.

Veiners (b). These stamps are called veiners because they are used to make the veins on leaves. They are excellent stamps for other sorts of designs, too. When a veiner is used on a leaf, it is usually tipped slightly so that one end goes in deeper, at the center of the leaf. In the picture, note shaders in the flower petals and veiners in the leaves.

Geometrics (c). These are really useful stamps; they make good borders, they can be used all by themselves to cover a whole area, and they combine with other stamps well. One special kind of geometric stamp is the basketweave. It makes the leather look woven. A trick to getting the basketweave even is to draw a light guideline with a ruler, at an angle, and stamp first one side of the line, then the other side, then the first side—use this as a guide for the rest of the stamping.

Outline Stamping or Inverted Carving. You can outline a design with stamps called backgrounders (d) so that the Acrylic Antique Finish makes the outline dark and leaves the design itself lighter. This is a good way to make mountains and clouds, for example. For these designs the swivel knife is not used at all.

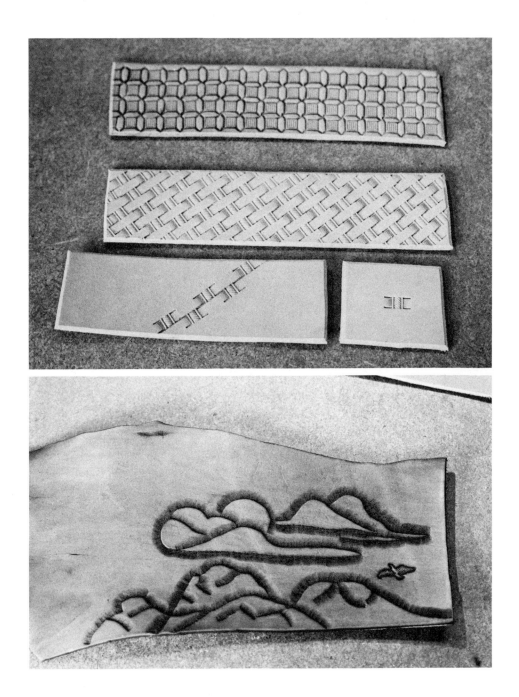

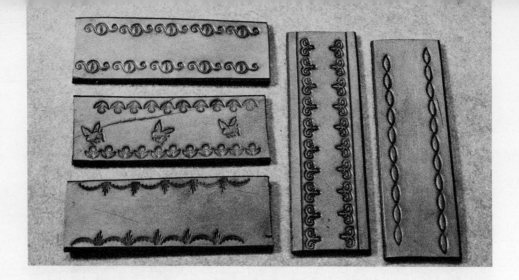

Before stamping your project, plan your design. Try your stamps scattered—all over the piece. Or stamp along the edges; draw a light pencil line, using a ruler, for a guideline. Or run dividers along the edge to make the guideline; do this lightly, or it will show. Dividers

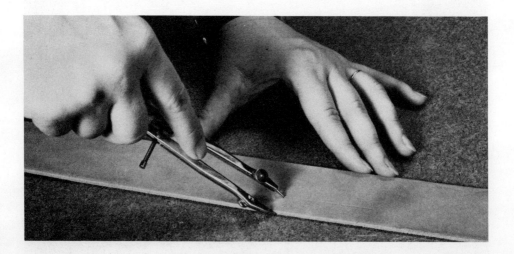

can also be used to "walk" along a piece to make evenly spaced points. Try stamping down the center line of your piece; draw a guideline first. Or start from a center point, or points, and build out. Choose one stamp to be the center, then see what might go around it. Or make a wavy swivel knife line and then add stamps—oak leaf and acorn, flowers and leaves, wheat, ducks on the waves . . .

Try putting the design or parts of it in different places on the project, not just in one place. For a purse, make the main design on the purse flap, but also add a small design of the same type on the shoulder strap and on the back of the purse. On a visor, the biggest part of the design is usually on the bill; put some of the same stamps on the buckle strap, too.

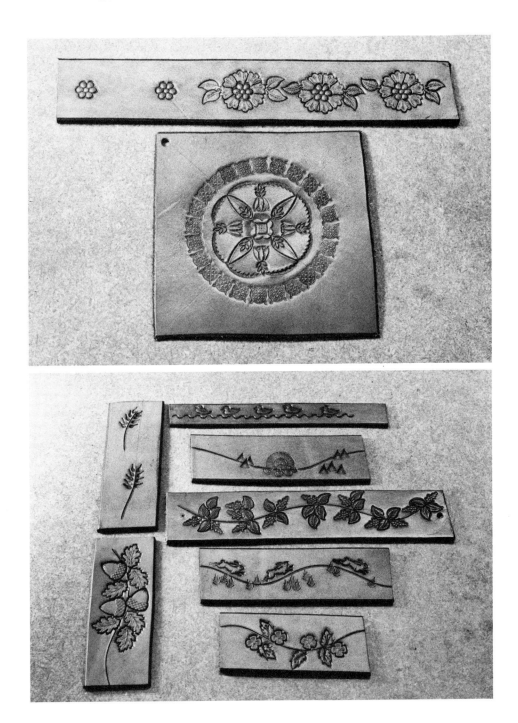

5.
Coloring Leather

You do not have to put anything on the leather at all—if you like the color the way it is when you buy it, leave it that way! Latigo and oak-tanned cowhide will darken with age; the latigo turns a beautiful golden tan, and oak-tanned usually turns a slightly reddish medium brown. If you do choose to color your leather, I suggest that you try putting it outside in the sun for several hours first. You can do this at any time—before you cut any pieces out, or after the edges are beveled and the holes punched. This will make the leather easier to color—dye and finish will go on more deeply and evenly.

All coloring should be done *after* stamping, and *before* putting the project together. If you stamp first, the finish will make the designs show up. And it's much easier to dye flat separate pieces than a laced-up thing.

Please note that dyes and finishes are poison; it's best to wash up soon after using them, keep them away from your mouth and eyes, use them in a well-ventilated area, and make sure they are well out of the reach of small children. If you have very sensitive skin or cuts on your hands, or you don't want Leatherworkers' Dirty Fingernails, wear rubber gloves.

There are three different ways to color leather—dye, Acrylic Antique Finish, and paint—and you can use any or all of them on your project. I recommend that you use the Finish (if you want to color the leather at all), either by itself, over dye, or under paint.

**LEATHER COLORERS' GOLDEN RULE:
TRY IT FIRST ON SCRAP!**

Leather Dye

Leather dye is watery thin. It comes in many colors—red, green, navy, black, yellow, purple, tan, spice, honey, chocolate, oxblood are a few examples. Dye sinks right into the leather; it doesn't make dark edges or show up the grain. It can be used to color a whole piece or small areas of a design. You can use dye by itself, but it looks better and lasts better with Acrylic Antique Finish over it. When you put Finish on top of dye, it changes the color somewhat, making it less bright, more even, and more interesting—the Finish shows up the grain of the leather.

The color you get when you use dye (or Finish) partly depends on the original color of the leather. For example, if your project is made out of yellow latigo, you can imagine what happens when you put blue dye on it! The result, of course, is green, since blue and yellow make green. Yellow latigo does make beautiful warm colors; that's one reason so many leatherworkers like it. If you find you like the yellow color base but you want to use oak-tanned cowhide for a project, dye the oak-tanned with yellow dye, and then dye and/or Finish the project any color you like. Experiment on a scrap of the same leather as your project. If you are using oak-tanned leather, dampen it before using dye; the dye will sink into the leather better.

Dye smells strong, so use it in a well-ventilated area. If you want to color the whole piece, fold a coarse cloth rag into a little bundle. (Don't use the dauber that comes with the bottle; it splatters.) Put some dye on the rag, and blot off the extra onto newspaper. Rub the rag on your leather. Keep building up the dye until you have the color you want. Let the piece dry several hours or more, then put on the Finish. Keep in mind that dye dries lighter than when you put it on.

If you want the stamping to be lighter than the rest, do the same thing as above, but blot most of the dye off the rag onto newspaper. Keep blotting it until it hardly shows on the paper. Then rub the rag lightly on the leather, and the dye will just hit the high spots, not sink down in the stamping. Let dry several hours. You can't use Finish on the front of this project, because it would darken the stamping, but it's a good idea to put Finish on the back and edges of the piece—carefully, and wipe off the excess.

For a really nice effect, choose a piece of latigo with a *lot* of grain showing, and use dye as above (blotting most of it off on newspaper)—let dry completely, then use Finish. The grain will show through.

To color areas of a carved design, pour a little of the dye into the bottle cap, and move the cap close to the place you're dyeing, with newspaper under it. With a small paintbrush, fill in the areas. Don't worry about getting the edges of the design perfectly even, since the Acrylic Antique Finish will make them all dark anyway. Use plenty of dye—go over the area a couple of times—because the dye dries lighter than it looks when it's wet. Let the piece dry for at least six hours, to make sure it doesn't smear. Then use the Finish.

Acrylic Antique Finish

If you want to use one type of coloring only, this is the kind to get. Try to get Acrylic Antique Finish, not just Antique Finish, because the non-acrylic kind does water spot, and nothing you put over it can stop it. The brand I recommend is Angelus.

Acrylic Antique Finish (sometimes called Finish) darkens the beveled edges, the stamping, and the back of the piece so they are darker than the rest, and it brings out the grain in the leather. It is thick——about like a milkshake—and comes in several shades of brown (red brown, cordovan, mahogany, light brown, etc.). It has wax and a sealer in it, so the finish won't water spot, and it can be buffed up to a glossy shine.

Here's the way to use Finish: *Smear it on really thick, and wipe it off.* First spread out some newspapers, and have ready kitchen-type paper towels (not the hard, scratchy school restroom kind) or soft rags. Try to get some shearling scraps for applying Finish, because it's a lot easier and you'll probably do a better job if you have them. Otherwise, try a damp sponge or a folded-up rag. Your project should be all cut out, edges beveled, holes punched, and any stamping done. Take one piece at a time. If it's oak-tanned, dampen with water. Oak-tanned leather is somewhat drier than latigo, and Finish tends to dry too fast (before you can wipe off the excess) unless you dampen the leather first.

Shake the bottle. Now, with a little scrap of shearling, smear on plenty of Finish. Turn the piece over and do the back, then turn the piece right side up and smear the Finish around on the front again. If the Finish looks like it's getting dry, put some more on.

Move the leather to a clean spot on the newspaper, take the paper towel, and wipe off the excess Finish. It works best if you wipe rather lightly, around and around in a circle, so that it doesn't streak. If it dries before you can get it off, or looks really dark and streaky—no problem, just put some more Finish on to loosen it up. If your paper towel gets all loaded up with Finish, move to a clean spot on the paper towel, or get a fresh one. Don't rub hard at all—the main thing is to get it on *thick* and wipe it off. You don't have to wipe off the back side. If the color you get isn't dark enough, do it again—but if you want very dark leather, you'll have to use a dye first. To get extra Finish out of the holes, slap the piece down onto a clean area of newspaper, then check to see if the front needs wiping off again.

Now move the piece to a separate spot to dry for a few minutes. Notice how the edges and stamping are dark, and the grain and other natural markings show up.

Acrylic Antique Finish is gooey, messy stuff. You can clean up your hands with soap and water; do it right away or you may have a little left here and there. If you get some on your clothes, just wash them as quickly as possible.

Leather Paint

Leather paint is acrylic paint, specially mixed so that it will stick to leather and not crack when the leather is bent. Unlike leather dye, paint does not sink in, but sits right on top. Paint should be applied after Acrylic Antique Finish and dye—it's the last thing. If you put it on first, the Finish or dye will smear it or take it off entirely.

Leather paint makes really bright colors, brighter than dye or Finish. It is best used for small areas only. You can get white, black, red, blue, yellow, green, orange, violet, and many others—and you can mix your own colors if you like. Mix tiny bits at a time, in the cap or in a water-color tray—a drop of this and a drop of that—and you can make fantastic colors!

Stir the paints well before using them, since the parts separate. Pour a *small* amount into the cap—it's easier to control how much you get on the brush that way. Carefully wipe your brush dry after rinsing it with water; even a small amount of water in the paint makes it look watery on the leather. Dip in the brush and get a tiny bit of paint, then color your design. It might need two coats.

If you let the paint dry, you can put another color on top of the first; for example, you might want to add black spots to a red ladybug, or some white highlights on a pink rose.

Be sure that the paint has a chance to dry thoroughly—twenty-four hours—before any rough use.

6.
Putting Your Project Together

Nearly always, this is the last step—put the pieces together after decorating and coloring.

Rivets

Rivets are an excellent way to fasten pieces of leather together. Use rivets when you want a permanent fastening (unlike snaps). They are most useful in projects where you need to hold together relatively small areas: to hold on a belt buckle, a key ring, a dog leash clip; to fasten a strap to a larger piece of leather, as in the knapsack and shoulder bag. Get solid brass Speedy Rivets (cap and post).

Here's how to put a rivet in. Punch #5 holes in the two pieces of leather you want to rivet together. Put in the rivet pieces—post (a) up through the bottom, and cap (b) on top—and squeeze them together a little with your fingers. Set the leather and rivet on your anvil, cap side

up, and use your metal hammer to *smash* the rivet flat. Don't be timid; the rivet really must be flat to hold the pieces together. If the top or bottom of the rivet is rounded or sticks out from the surface at all, you didn't hit hard enough—put it back on the anvil and give it a few more whacks.

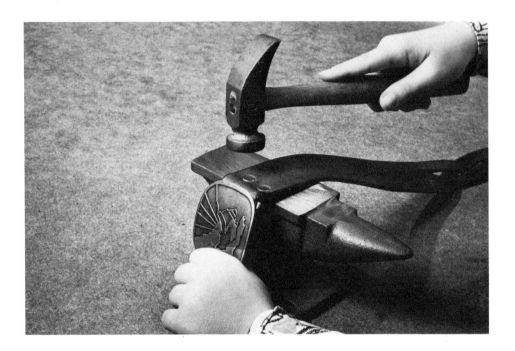

If you set a rivet properly, it will not come out. Just in case you put one in the wrong place, here's how to take it out. Pound a nail set (or a big nail if you don't have a nail set) through the top side of the rivet until the two parts are pushed apart. (This ruins the rivet, of course.)

Chicago Post and Screw

This two-part fastener can be used instead of a rivet, in a place where you would like to be able to remove the fastener without destroying it. To use a Chicago post and screw, punch holes in the two leather pieces (the hole should be a little bigger than the one a #5 punch makes, so just enlarge the hole slightly with your punch). Put in the two parts and screw them together. You can do this with your fingers, usually, or use a dime or screwdriver. Chicago posts are good for belts, because they

are not as bulky as belt snaps, and the buckle can be changed later, without the use of tools.

Snaps

Use these when you want to open and close the two leather pieces frequently—on a wristband or coin purse, for example.

Get the best kind of snaps: solid brass, four parts to each snap— Durable Dot for heavy leather (eight-ounce and over), and Baby Durable Dot for seven-ounce and under. Look for the two parts which have a rounded shape—they are the two top parts, the button and socket. The two flat-bottomed ones are the bottom parts, the stud and eyelet.

Punch holes in the leather where you want to set the snap. For the *top* part, put the snap parts—button (a) and socket (b)—in the leather.

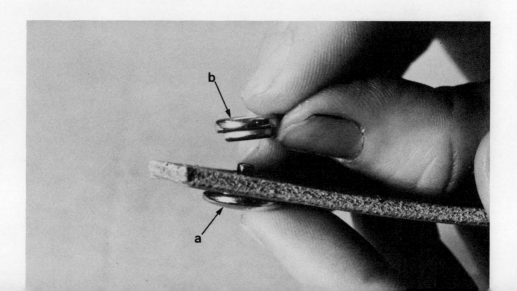

The button is on the smooth side of the leather. Put the small rounded "anvil" on your big anvil, and put the leather on the anvil, smooth side down. Look at the snap setter, and you will see a hole at each end; one is bigger. Use the big hole on the top of the snap. Put in the pin and hit the pin with the metal hammer several times—not a hard whack, but

TOP

several taps. Take away the setter, and see if the snap is on securely. If not, put back the setter, and hit it again.

For the *bottom* part, you don't need the round anvil, since the bottom parts are flat. Put in the stud (a) and eyelet (b); the eyelet is on the smooth side of the leather. Put the leather on the anvil right side up, and use the small hole end of the setter.

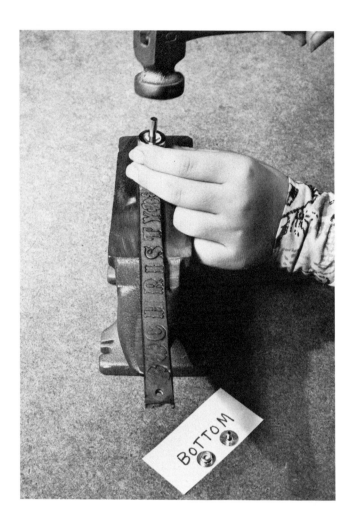

Glue

Glue is best used only when you are going to have another kind of fastener also; usually it can't hold well enough by itself. However, you might use glue by itself to turn up the hem of a vest, skirt, or pouch, or to cement a new rubber heel on a pair of sandals. Rubber cement is the kind to get. It comes in a small tube or a can with a brush—the can with a brush is easier to use.

To do a good job: If the area to be glued is smooth, scratch and rough it up as best you can with sandpaper. Spread a thin, even layer of rubber cement over both surfaces you want to put together. Make sure the cement goes all the way out to the edges. Then wait about twenty minutes before you put the layers together. Sounds strange, but that's the way it works. If you can put the two parts in the sun while you are waiting, they will stick better. After about twenty minutes—when the glue is no longer wet, but just sticky—put the two pieces together. Squeeze and smooth them with your hands, especially around the edges. It's also good to tap everything flat, gently, with the metal hammer.

Lacing

Lacing means putting the parts together with leather strips; sewing is done with thread. You can choose either method to put any pieces of leather together, and the kind of stitch you use depends on your preference as well. For your first several projects, use the method suggested in the directions; then you'll have a better idea of the stitches and which ones you like to use.

First, punch the holes for the lacing to go through. Lacing looks and holds best when the holes are spaced relatively close together. For latigo lacing, holes about ½ inch apart are good. For the thinner calf lacing, I use a 5-to-the-inch stitchmarker to space the holes.

For a really fine-looking project, the lacing should fit the holes. Since lacing does tend to stretch out a little, I choose lacing that is just a bit larger than the hole. For example, use lacing that is $^3/_{16}$ inch wide for the holes you'll make with your $^5/_{32}''$ punch (that's $^1/_{32}$ inch bigger than the holes).

How long a piece of lacing do you need? For a running stitch, use a piece about 1½ times as long as the seam, for whipstitch about 3½ times, and for cross stitch about 5 times. These are not exact measurements, because it depends on the spacing of the holes and how tightly you lace; if in doubt, use a little extra.

Wax the lacing to make it slip through the holes easily. Just pull the dyed lace over a piece of paraffin (the kind you get in the supermarket for candles and jelly glasses) or beeswax or even an old candle end. Be sure to keep the wax away from any undyed leather, because even tiny bits of wax will make the leather not take dye.

Use a lacing needle. Cut a long, narrow point on the end of the lacing and screw the needle on as far as it will go. If you don't get it on firmly on the first try, unscrew it, cut a new tapered end on the lacing, and try again. If you should happen to pull the lacing out of the needle, leaving a bit of lacing in the end, hold the needle over a candle flame (hold it with pliers so your hand doesn't get burned) until the bit of lacing burns out. It's nearly impossible to pick it out.

Pull the lacing snug as you go—pull on each stitch. The best way is to poke the lacing needle through the holes, take hold of the *lacing,* and draw it almost all the way through. Don't hold onto the needle when pulling it through. Then move your fingers close to the project, make sure the lacing is straight and not twisted, and pull it through the rest of the way. Keep checking as you go to make sure you haven't missed any holes; it's no fun to have to pull stitches out.

Twisted lacing? Twisted lacing looks terrible, and it's easy to avoid. Just straighten out the lacing each time before you put in the needle, and check it before you finally pull it snug. This is much easier than trying to straighten the lacing out after it is pulled tight.

What about the ends of the lacing? With latigo lacing, you can tie a single knot in the end; the knot will be big enough so it won't pull through the holes. For calf lacing, a single knot probably isn't big enough and might pull through. Sometimes you can tie two lacing ends together in a square knot. If there is no other lacing end to tie to, try lacing backward a stitch or two, into the same holes you just used, and tie the lace to itself on the back side of the project.

There are many, many lacing stitches. The projects in this book use just three: the running stitch, the cross stitch, and the whipstitch, described under sewing. Fancy lacing stitches are fun to do and very decorative; see the bibliography on page 128 for some good books on lacing.

Running stitch: One piece of leather overlaps the other; both pieces of leather have the top grain side up. Pull the lacing out the first hole, in the next, out the third, and so on, going through both layers of leather each time.

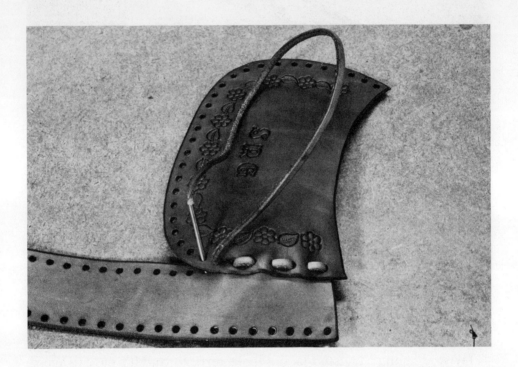

Cross stitch: Put the two pieces of leather side by side, not overlapping, with the edges to be laced just touching. It's very helpful to have two lacing needles for this stitch—one for each end of the lacing, as shown—but if you have only one, you can switch it back and forth from one end of the lacing to the other as you go. Start with the middle of the lacing in the first holes; pull one end of the lacing through each hole (a). Then, with one needle, cross over to the other side, and go in the second hole. With the other needle, cross over and go in the second hole on that side (b). Make the lacing cross, on the back, to its original side, and come out the third hole up. Contine this way (c). Tie the lacing ends in a square knot when the seam is finished.

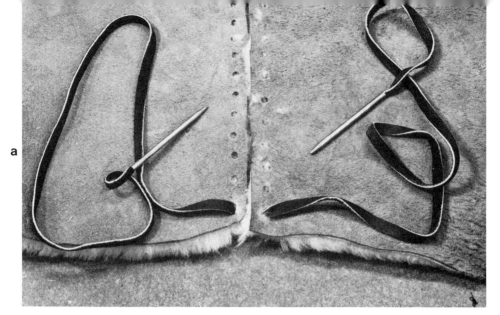

a

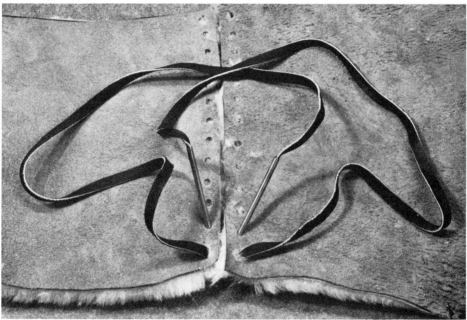

b

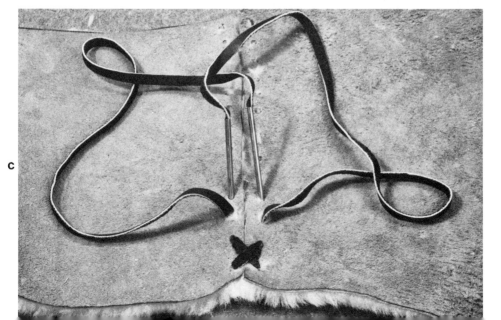

c

Sewing

On soft leather you can sew with a glovers' needle (sharp point) and waxed nylon thread, without punching any holes first. (The thread comes already waxed; you won't have to wax it.) If you have trouble threading the needle, cut off the end of the thread to make a point. (You won't be able to make it very pointed; just cut it at an angle.) Put the thread end on your anvil and tap it gently with the hammer. Since the thread is waxed, this will stick the end together better and make it easier to put through the eye of the needle.

The whipstitch is a good one to use. In the whipstitch, the thread goes through the two layers of leather, over the edges, and through again. Sometimes the layers are placed with the right sides (outsides) together, sewn, then turned right side out, as in the pouch and knapsack. (The whipstitch can also be used with the holes punched first, and it can be done with lacing as well as with thread.) Keep the stitches close together so they will look good and hold well. If you have any trouble getting the needle through the layers, push the end of the needle against the workbench or other hard surface to help it almost all the way through, then pull. This way, you won't hurt yourself on the sharp edge of the needle.

For stiff or thick leather, mark the hole spacing (about five holes to the inch), punch holes with a small-sized punch (#0, $^1/_{16}''$), and sew the seam using waxed nylon thread and harness needles (dull point).

Here is an excellent stitch—the double running stitch or saddle stitch. In this one, the thread goes through each hole twice. Use a length of thread about three times the length of the seam. Put a harness needle on *each end* of the thread, and start with the middle of the piece of thread in the first hole—so that one needle is out the front and one is out the back (a). With one of the needles, do a running stitch for a few stitches—in and out and in and out, not skipping any holes (b). Then

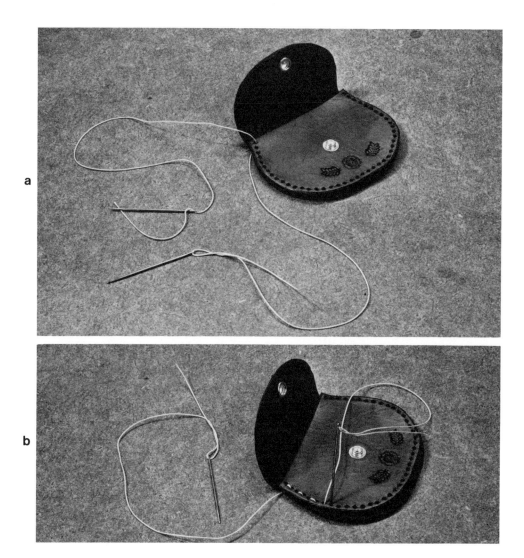

a

b

drop that needle and pick up the other one. Do a running stitch with *that* needle, going through the same holes again—filling up the spaces left by the first needle (c, d). Do only a few stitches at a time with each needle, so you can pull the sewing tight. Sewing first with one needle and then with the other, sew to the end of the seam.

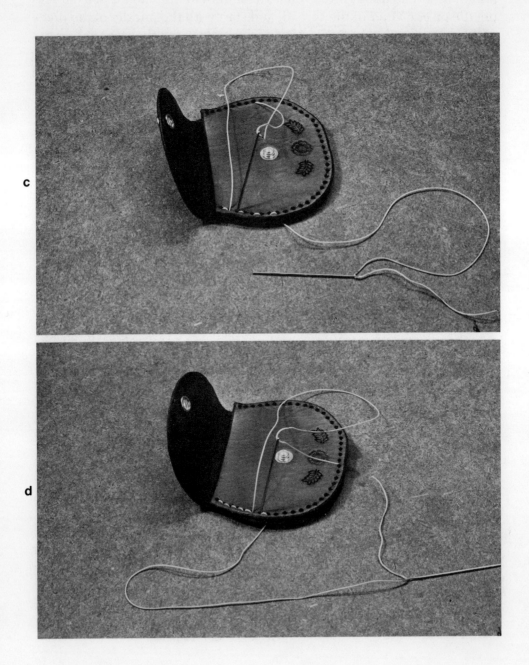

c

d

With the double running stitch, both threads end up in the same place, so you can run the top one through a hole to the back side and tie the two together in a tight square knot. Then tap the knot with the metal hammer. Tap the seam gently with the hammer to flatten it.

Buffing

When the pieces are together, you're finished! If you are working with latigo or oak-tanned leather, you might want to buff up the project to make it shine a little. You can polish it with a rag or buff it with a shoe brush. For a really glossy look, if you like, you can put on a little wax and buff. Wait several hours to do this, so the Finish won't smear. Use a neutral (no color) shoe cream like Propert's or Meltonian brand (don't use shoe polish; it comes off). Put on tiny dabs (you can use your fingers), then buff away until you get a beautiful, natural-looking shine.

When leather is exposed frequently to sun, water, or wear, it tends to dry out and crack. To help prevent this, apply neat's-foot oil or silicone oil about once a month, depending on how much the article is used. Lexol is a very good brand of oil to use. You can put it on with your fingers. For areas larger than a few square inches, I like to apply it this way, for a thin, even coat: Dampen a rag with warm water, squeeze out the excess water, pour on a little Lexol, and squeeze again to coat the rag evenly. Rub the rag lightly on the article several times. This treatment not only preserves leather, it also makes it look better, clearing up small scratches. The oil may darken the leather a little—sometimes temporarily, sometimes it stays darker. (Don't use oil on suede; it gums down the nap.)

7.
Projects

Pendant

MATERIALS
6–7 oz. latigo or oak-tanned cowhide, piece about 2″ × 3″
Finish; dye, paint if desired
yarn, cord, or thong for hanging pendant

TOOLS
cutter
edger

#5 punch
for drive punch: mallet, anvil, rubber soling material
decorating tools (stamps, etc.)
for stamping: mallet; anvil or marble

1. Cut the leather to the shape you want. (Plan the shape on paper first if you like, then draw around pattern onto the leather.)
2. Bevel the edges.
3. Punch a hole at the top, to hang the pendant from.
4. Decorate with stamps, holes, swivel knife, whatever you like! Dampen oak-tanned before stamping or carving.
5. Use Acrylic Antique Finish—smear it on *thick*, then wipe it off. Let dry about twenty minutes. Color the stamped places with paint if desired.
6. Let the pendant dry thoroughly—several hours if it has been painted—then buff it up.
7. Put in a piece of thong, yarn, or string, and tie the ends in a knot.

Barrette

MATERIALS

8–9 oz. latigo or oak-tanned cowhide, piece about 3″ × 5″. Barrette can be made out of 6–7 oz. leather but will hold its shape better when made of 8–9 oz.

Finish; dye, paint if desired
stick—about 4½″ of ¼″ dowel or a candy-apple stick or a twig

TOOLS
cutter
edger
⅝″ drive punch (optional) or #5 punch
for drive punch: mallet, anvil, rubber soling material
decorating tools (stamps, etc.)
for stamping: mallet; anvil or marble

1. Trace the pattern and cut it out. Or make your own pattern by folding a piece of paper in four and cutting a shape you like. Draw around the pattern onto the leather. Mark where the holes go, but do not cut them out.
2. Cut out the barrette.
3. Bevel the edges.
4. Punch the holes. If you don't have a ⅝″ drive punch, you can nibble out a hole with your #5 punch—it won't be perfect, but it will work.
5. Decorate as desired. Dampen oak-tanned before stamping or carving.
6. Color and finish as desired.
7. Buff up the barrette when dry.
8. You can put points on the stick with a pencil sharpener (don't make it too sharp), and color it with Acrylic Antique Finish or leather dye if you want it to be dark.

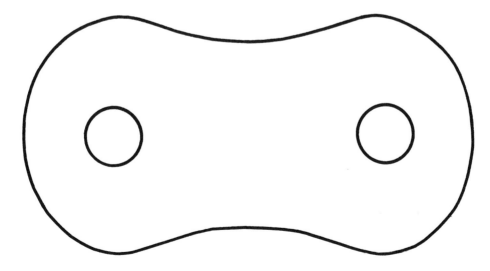

Light Switch Plate

MATERIALS
4–7 oz. yellow latigo or oak-tanned cowhide, piece big
   enough for the pattern
Finish; dye, paint if desired

TOOLS
cutter
edger
#5 punch, slot punch (optional)
for drive punch: mallet, anvil, rubber soling material
decorating tools (stamps, etc.)
for stamping: mallet; anvil or marble

1. Trace the pattern, and cut it out. Check to make sure that the size
   and the screw holes are right for your switch. Or make a pattern
   yourself. The outline can be just about any shape, but keep in mind
   that a very complicated shape will be more difficult to cut than a
   simple one.
2. Hold the pattern on the leather, and draw around it with a pencil.
   Mark the holes.
3. Bevel the edges.
4. Punch the holes. The slot for the switch can be made with a slot

punch, moving the punch over and punching again to make a wider hole. Or make holes with the #5 punch at the ends of the slot, and connect the holes with the cutter.

5. Decorate the leather. Dampen oak-tanned before stamping or carving.
6. Color and finish as desired.
7. Wait until the Finish and paint are dry—an hour or so—then buff up.

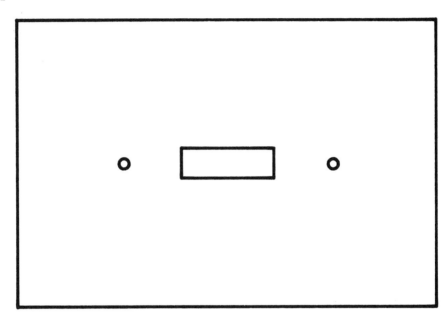

Key Ring

MATERIALS
6–7 oz. yellow latigo, piece big enough for the pattern
metal key ring
solid brass rivet
Finish; dye, paint if desired

TOOLS
cutter
edger
#5 punch

for drive punch: mallet, rubber soling material
decorating tools (stamps, etc.)
for stamping: mallet; marble (optional)
metal hammer
anvil

1. Trace and cut out the pattern. Or to make your own pattern, get a piece of paper about 2½ inches wide and about 4 inches long, and fold it in half the long way. Draw and cut out a "half key ring" shape, then unfold the paper—cutting the pattern from folded paper will give you an even shape, with both sides the same. Make sure you leave the top part long enough to go around the ring, as in our pattern. Draw the pattern onto the leather, using a pencil.
2. Cut out the leather piece.
3. Bevel the edges, front and back.
4. Wrap the leather around the key ring, so you can tell where to make the holes for the rivet. Punch the holes. You can punch both layers at once, with the leather wrapped around the ring, or you can mark

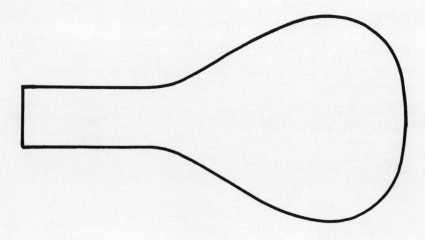

the holes with a pencil, take away the ring, and punch the layers separately.

5. Stamp, or otherwise decorate.
6. Use Acrylic Antique Finish. When the Finish is dry (about fifteen minutes), paint if desired. Wait again after painting, so you won't smear the paint when you put in the rivet.
7. Wrap the leather around the key ring, put in the rivet, put the whole thing on your anvil, and smash the rivet flat with the metal hammer. Let the key ring itself hang off the side of the anvil when you pound the rivet, so you won't hit the ring.
8. When the key ring is thoroughly dry, you can buff it up if you like.

Wristband

MATERIALS
6–7 oz. yellow latigo, strip about ¾″ wide
Finish; dye, paint if desired
solid brass snap

TOOLS
cutter
edger

#5 punch
for drive punch: mallet, rubber soling material
decorating tools (stamps, etc.)
for stamping: mallet, marble (optional)
snap setter
metal hammer
anvil

1. Measure the wrist, and add about ¾ inch for overlap. Add more if you want the band to fit loosely. (For a braided wristband, add about 1¼ inches to the wrist measurement.) Cut the leather strip to length.
2. Bevel the edges, front and back.
3. Punch holes for the snap—one in each end.
4. Decorate however you like—stamps, holes, swivel knife, V-gouge. Or for a braided wristband, see directions for braided belt.
5. Use Acrylic Antique Finish, making sure you darken all the edges and the back. Wipe off the extra Finish. Let the wristband dry a few minutes, then paint it if you want to. Let the paint dry for fifteen minutes or so, so that it won't smear while you're doing the snap.
6. Set the snap.
7. After a couple of hours, the paint will be really dry, and you can buff the wristband to a glossy shine.

Mirror or Picture Frame

MATERIALS

6–7 oz. latigo or oak-tanned cowhide, piece big enough for
    the pattern
Finish; dye, paint if desired
cardboard
2¾″ × 4″ mirror, or a picture or photo
rubber cement
8″ or so of thong, cord, etc. for hanging

TOOLS

cutter
edger
#5 punch
for drive punch: mallet, anvil, rubber soling material
decorating tools (stamps, etc.)
for stamping: mallet; anvil or marble

1. Trace and cut out the pattern, if you want this size and shape—or
   make your own pattern. To do that, cut paper to the size you want.

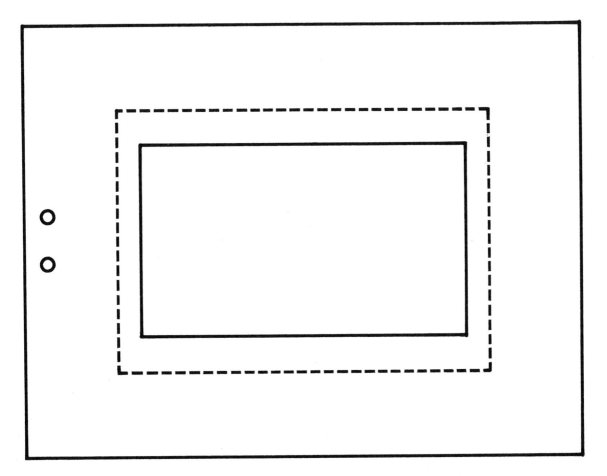

Fold the paper in four and cut the shape. Cut the hole for the mirror or picture, making the hole smaller than the mirror or picture.

2. Hold the pattern on the leather by weighting it down with something heavy, like your anvil, while you draw around the pattern with a pencil.

3. Cut out the leather piece. Cut the hole for the mirror or picture.

4. Bevel all the cut edges.

5. Punch the holes for hanging.

6. Decorate the leather. You might plan a design on the paper pattern first, and transfer the design to the leather by pressing through the paper to the leather with something like a pencil, a nail, a modeling tool, or an awl. You won't have to press hard enough to cut the paper, just enough to transfer the design. Dampen oak-tanned before stamping or carving.

7. Color and finish as desired. This is one project where it's a good idea *not* to put any Finish on the back side, because the glue will work better if you don't.

8. *For a picture or photograph:* Cut out a piece of cardboard, about ⅛ inch smaller all around than the leather (so it won't show). Punch holes for hanging in the cardboard—put the leather over the cardboard and mark through the hanging holes. Punch holes in the cardboard at the marked spots.

Try out the placement of the picture before gluing it down: put the picture on the cardboard, then put the leather on top. Adjust the picture so that it looks the way you want it to, then take away the leather and make pencil guidelines on the cardboard, around the picture. Glue the picture to the cardboard, then glue the leather on top. Put in the thong or cord, and tie a knot. Buff up the leather.

9. *For a mirror:* You'll notice that a mirror is not flat, like a photograph, and if you did a mirror the same as a picture, there would be a bump showing. So cut out *two* pieces of cardboard, both about ⅛ inch smaller than the leather, all around. Set the mirror on one of these cardboard pieces and draw around it. Cut on the lines to make a hole just the size of the mirror, so the mirror can fit right into it. It doesn't have to be perfect, because the leather will cover it. As in step 8, punch holes for hanging in both pieces of cardboard.

Now glue the cardboard with the hole to the cardboard without a hole, glue in the mirror, and glue the leather on top. Put the thong or cord through the hanging holes, tie a knot, and buff up the mirror frame.

Coin Purse

MATERIALS
4-7 oz. latigo or oak-tanned cowhide, piece big enough for
   the pattern
Finish; dye, paint if desired
waxed nylon thread
Baby Durable Dot brass snap

TOOLS
cutter
edger
#0 punch, #5 punch
for drive punch: mallet, rubber soling material
decorating tools (stamps, etc.)
for stamping: mallet, marble (optional)
snap setter
metal hammer
anvil
2 harness needles

1. Trace and cut out the pattern, put it on the smooth side of the
   leather, and draw the pattern onto the leather with a pencil.
2. Cut out the two leather pieces.
3. Bevel the edges, front and back.
4. Punch the holes—#0 for the sewing holes, and #5 for the snap
   holes.
5. Put on the design, if you want one, with stamps, swivel knife,

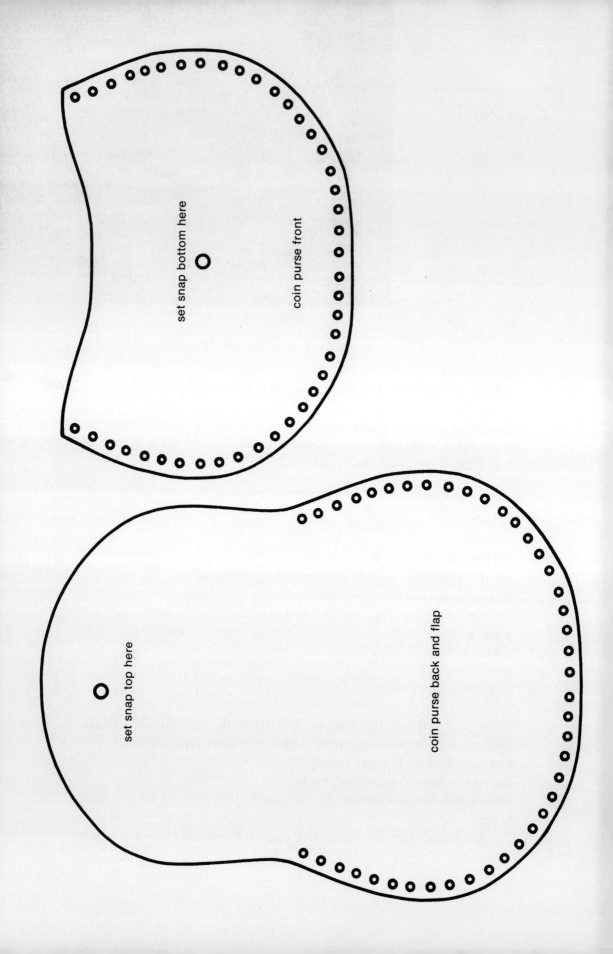

set snap bottom here

coin purse front

set snap top here

coin purse back and flap

V-gouge, etc. If you are using oak-tanned leather, dampen the pieces before stamping or carving.

6. Coloring is next. When the Finish is dry, add paint if you like, with a tiny brush. Let paint dry before setting snap.

7. Set the snap. Note that you set the snap before sewing the coin purse together, because it would be hard to get the snap setter inside the purse after it is sewn.

8. Sew the pieces together. Use the double running stitch, page 61. At the end of the seam, get both threads to the same side of the purse, and tie a square knot.

9. Put the coin purse on the anvil, and gently tap the sewing flat, using the metal hammer.

10. Buff the coin purse with a shoe brush or rag, to polish it up a bit.

Tool Board

Here's a good way to keep your tools handy and safe. Make it for leatherworking tools, woodworking tools, drawing tools, or just about any kind.

leather straps—4–9 oz. latigo or oak-tanned cowhide, ½″ to 1″
   wide
a piece of plywood (½″ or ⅝″ thick) or other wood, big enough
   to lay your tools out on—the one in the picture is 20″ × 21″
shoe tacks (the kind that clinch) or carpet tacks—long enough
   to go through both the wood and the leather

TOOLS
felt pen
cutter
metal hammer
anvil

1. Gather together the tools you are going to hang on the board. Lay
   the board flat, and arrange the tools the way you want them. Use a
   felt pen to draw around each tool onto the wood. This way, you'll
   know instantly where a tool goes when you're putting it away.
2. Put one of the tools in its place, and wrap a piece of strap over it,
   where you want to hang it. Don't forget that if the tool has a tapered
   shape, the wider part has to be above the strap, or the strap won't
   hold it up. Mark and cut the strap to the correct length. Put the strap
   over the tool again, and mark with pencil where the strap ends come
   to on the wood. Take away the tool. Set the board on the anvil so
   that the anvil is right under the place where you will attach the
   strap. Using a metal hammer, pound a tack through the leather and
   through the wood, onto the anvil. The anvil will clinch the tack and
   make it hold. Then tack down the other end. You can use a separate
   piece of strap for each tool, or you can put tools in a row, using a

longer strap, with tacks in between the tools. For very small tools, or ones that won't hang that way, you might tack a leather pocket to the wood. This would be good for lacing and sewing needles, for example.

3. The tool board can be simply leaned up against a wall, or it can be hung on the wall by a leather thong.

Pouch

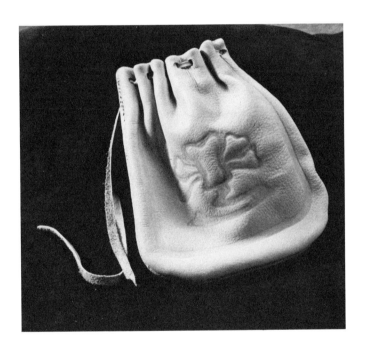

MATERIALS

2–2½ oz. chrome-tanned leather or suede, enough for two of the pattern pieces (take the pattern with you when you go to buy the leather)

materials for decorating—beads for drawstring ends, different colored leather or suede, etc. (optional)

waxed nylon thread—5 yards is plenty

rubber cement

lacing for the drawstring, or enough of the soft leather to cut your own—about 2 feet of lacing is plenty

mark these holes but do not punch them until hem has been glued down

cut 2 from leather

TOOLS
cutter
#5 punch
for drive punch: mallet, rubber soling material
electric pen (optional)
#000 glovers' needle (sharp point)
paper stapler (optional)
metal hammer
anvil

1. Trace and cut out the paper pattern. Hold it in place on the leather with something heavy, and draw around it with a pencil. Mark the holes at the same time.
2. Cut out the two pouch pieces.
3. Decorate the pouch as you like. Remember that chrome-tanned leather won't take stamping and carving. Electric pen often works well on soft leather—try it on a scrap—or you might sew or glue on different colored shapes, or do some fancy lacing on the front. Or, of course, you can leave it plain!
4. Place the pieces with right sides together, and whipstitch around the pouch, leaving the top edge open. Use waxed thread and a glovers' needle, and keep the stitches quite close together for strength. To keep the pieces from sliding around while you are sewing, you can use a regular paper stapler to "pin" them together in several places. Remove staples after sewing by carefully prying them open.
5. Spread rubber cement on the top two inches of the *wrong* side of the pouch. Let the glue dry for about twenty minutes, then turn down the hem (1 inch) and tap it flat with the metal hammer, on the anvil. Turn the pouch right side out. You can also tap the sewing flat.
6. Punch the holes, and thread in the drawstring.

Shearling Hat

MATERIALS

shearling suede (chrome-tanned sheepskin, suede on one side, wool on the other side), enough for three of the pattern pieces (take the pattern with you when you go to buy the leather)

10 feet of ¼″ lacing, about 2–3 oz. chrome-tanned leather or suede

TOOLS

cutter

#5 punch

for drive punch: anvil, mallet, rubber soling material

lacing needle for ¼″ lacing (2 needles for greater convenience)

1. Trace the pattern, cut it out, and tape the two parts together. Punch holes in the paper pattern. Paper is not as easy to punch with a leather punch as leather is, so put a piece of scrap leather under the paper, and punch through both.
2. Place the pattern on the suede, hold it there with a heavy object, and draw around the pattern with a soft pencil. Mark the holes, too. If you can't get the pencil to mark on the suede, use a pen—but make sure you're drawing in the right place, since you can't erase the pen marks! Draw three of the pattern pieces.
3. Cut out the three pieces.
4. Punch the holes.

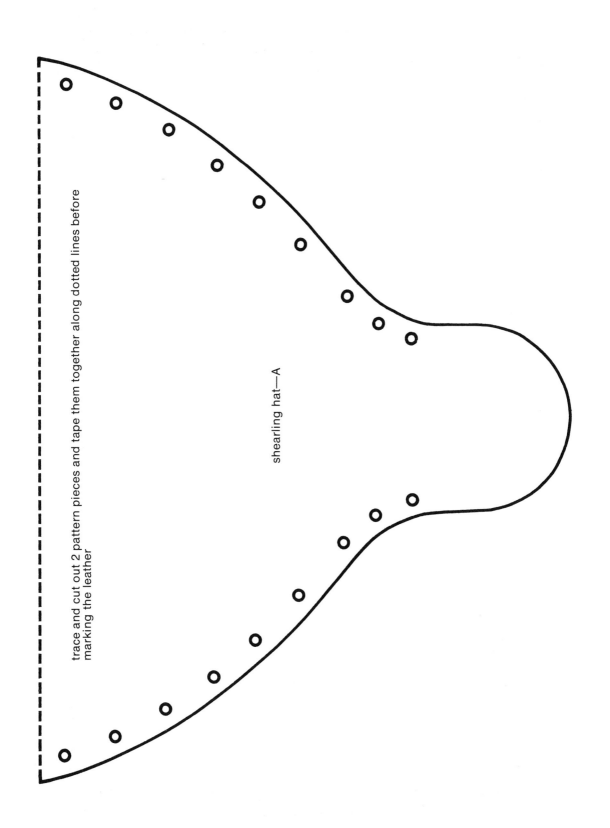

trace and cut out 2 pattern pieces and tape them together along dotted lines before marking the leather

shearling hat—A

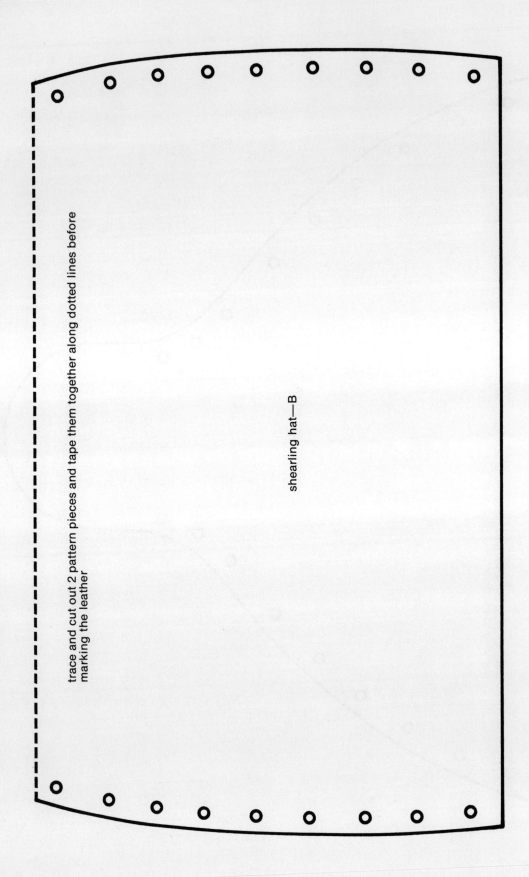

trace and cut out 2 pattern pieces and tape them together along dotted lines before marking the leather

shearling hat—B

5. Cut the 10-foot piece of lacing into three equal pieces, one for each seam. Lace the hat pieces together, using a cross stitch (see page 58). Start at the top or bottom, with the middle of the lace in the first holes. Tie the lacing ends in a square knot, and tuck the knot inside the hat. Turn up the brim. At first, the little pieces on the top of the hat stick straight up, but later they will turn down and show the furry side.

Kirigami Candle or Plant Hanger

This project looks complicated, but it isn't. It is easy to do *if you read the instructions!* "Kirigami" means "paper-cutting" in Japanese, and the pattern is made by cutting folded paper, as you can see. After you have made a few of these, you will see how the pattern works, and perhaps you'll want to make larger ones by adding rings or by folding paper and making a new pattern.

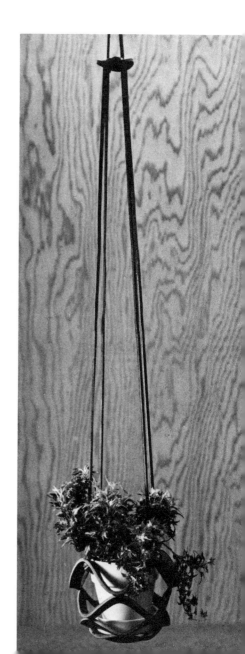

MATERIALS

about 7 oz. retanned cowhide. Dark brown waxhide (a retanned cowhide with lots of wax and oil) is best, because it
cuts easily and doesn't need dye or finish. You can also use
latigo. Take the pattern with you when you go to buy the
leather

about 9 feet of $5/32''$ lacing to match the main piece of leather
for hanging the kirigami

masking tape

TOOLS

razor cutter

#5 punch

for drive punch: mallet, anvil, rubber soling material

a piece of wood at least 1 foot square to cut on

a nail

metal hammer

1. Trace the pattern, and cut out the paper circle—don't cut the slits in
   the pattern.
2. Tape the pattern to the leather piece with masking tape. For this
   project, the pattern must not move even a little, or the slits will be
   placed wrong. Mark through the pattern onto the leather with your
   pencil; mark all the lines and holes. Make sure you get *all* the lines,
   since it would be hard to put the pattern back in the right place if
   you miss one! Mark the outside ring around the pattern, too.
3. Take away the pattern. Put the leather on the piece of wood, and
   drive the nail through the exact center of the leather, into the wood.
   The leather can pivot or spin around the nail, and that's what will
   make it easy for you to cut.
4. Check your razor cutter to make sure you have a good blade in it. I
   always put in a new blade for this project.
   Start cutting from the *outside* circle. Sink the blade into a place on
   the outside circle, through the leather into the wood, and start
   slowly pulling the *leather*. Keep the cutter straight up and down,
   and don't move it, just pull the leather. The cutter will cut right on
   your pencil line, in a perfect circle. On the next ring, where the
   pencil line stops, pick up the cutter—and put it back down where
   the line starts again. Cut all the slits this way, and cut out the center
   circle. Then pull the nail out.

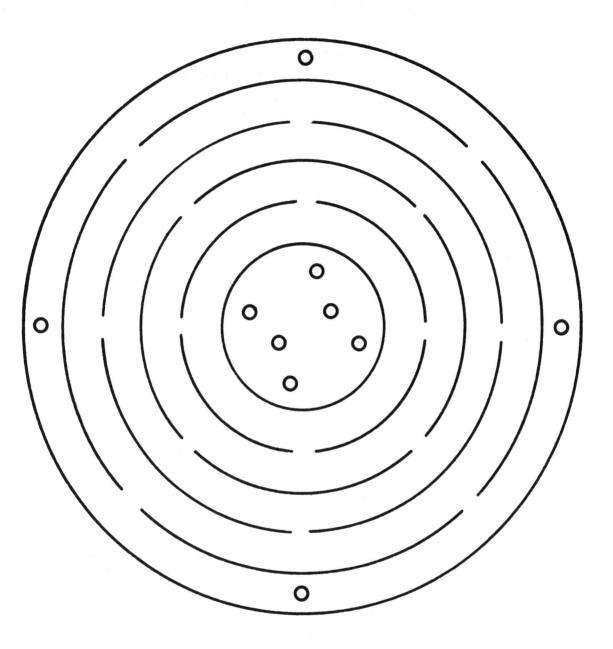

5. Punch all the holes.
6. Cut a one-foot piece of lacing. Push the ends through the two center holes in the small circle, and tie single knots on the underside. This makes the "topknot" for the hanger. If you have any trouble pushing the lacing through the holes, cut a slanted end on the lacing, and make the holes a tiny bit bigger with the punch.

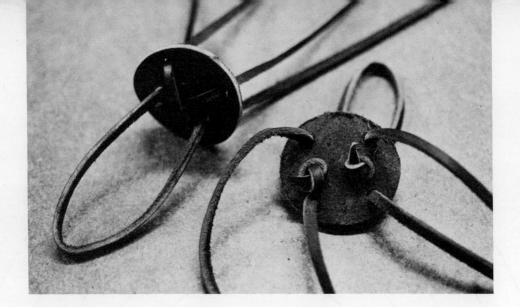

7. Cut the rest of the lacing in half, so you have two pieces about 4 feet long. It doesn't matter exactly how long they are, as long as they are the same. Push the two laces through the holes in the "topknot." Then put each end through a hole in the basket part. Tie a single knot in each. Adjust the laces to make them hang evenly, and pull on the bottom to stretch the basket part into shape.

Belt

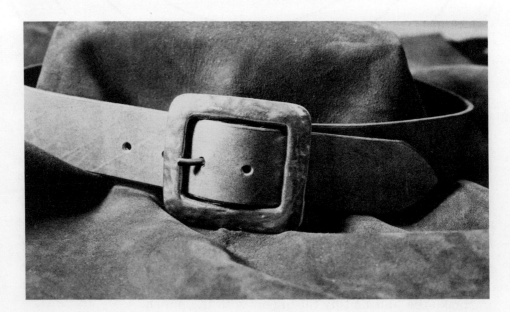

buckle, with or without a tongue. When you buy your materials, choose the buckle first, so you can get the leather to fit
it

about 8 oz. latigo or oak-tanned cowhide, a strip wide enough
to fit the buckle and about 3½ to 4 feet long, depending on
waist measurement (see steps 1 and 2)

Finish; dye, paint if desired

2 rivets or ¼" Chicago posts

TOOLS
cutter
edger
#5 punch, slot punch (optional)
for drive punch: mallet, rubber soling material
decorating tools (stamps, etc.)
for stamping: mallet, marble (optional)
metal hammer
anvil

1. First, measure the person you are going to make the belt for. Measure right where the belt will be worn. If you absolutely cannot
measure the person, since it's a surprise or something, you can use
the pants size—but to be safe, add one or two inches. Pants sizes
almost always turn out to be smaller than the person's actual measurement.

2. To the measurement, add 7½ inches. Cut the belt strip off at that
length. For example, if the person measures 28 inches around,
where the belt will be worn, add 7½ inches, and cut the belt strip off
at 35½ inches.

3. With a pencil, draw a point on one end of the belt strip. Cut the
point.

4. Bevel the edges of the belt strip, front and back.

5. Decorate the belt with stamps, swivel knife, etc. If you are using
oak-tanned leather, dampen it before stamping or carving. It's a
good idea to try out the design you plan to use on the scrap you cut
off.

6. Use dyes, Finish, paints to color the belt. You don't need to wait
until your oak-tanned belt is dry before dyeing it—the dyes actually

work better when the leather is damp. Let the belt dry about an hour before putting on the buckle, to make sure it doesn't smear.

7. Put on the buckle.

If the buckle has a tongue (a), punch a slot in the belt end for the tongue to go through. Make the slot in the middle of the strip, about 1½ inches from the end. It should be about 1 inch long. If you don't have a slot punch, you can nibble a slot with your #5 punch, or you can punch a hole in each end of the slot and connect the holes with the cutter. Wrap the belt around the buckle, with the tongue in the slot. If you are using oak-tanned leather for the belt, dampen the

buckle end of the belt when you wrap it around the buckle, if it isn't damp already. This will make the belt fold nicely around the buckle. Check to make sure that the buckle is on the right way before putting in the rivets or Chicago posts. If you use Chicago posts, you can change the buckle later. Chicago posts usually need larger holes than rivets, so just make the holes a little bigger with your punch. If you do use rivets, hold the buckle off the side of the anvil when you pound, so you won't hit the buckle and split the leather.

If the buckle does not have a tongue (b), you don't need to make a slot. Just wrap the belt end around the buckle (dampen it if it's oak-tanned) and make sure it's in the right way. Then punch holes and put in the rivets or Chicago posts.

8. Punch the holes on the other end. Make at least three holes, about one inch apart. The best way to tell where to put the holes is to put the belt on the person and mark where they should go. If you can't do that, measure along the belt to the person's waist measurement (measuring from the end of the buckle) and punch a hole at that spot. When you can't try on the belt to mark the holes, you'd better punch four or five holes, maybe two on either side of the measurement. If the #5 holes are too small for the buckle tongue, just nibble them a tiny bit bigger with your punch.

9. Belts look especially good when they are buffed up with a shoe brush or rag. Make sure the belt is dry before buffing. You can apply a tiny bit of neutral shoe cream before you brush the belt, if you want it really glossy.

Braided Belt

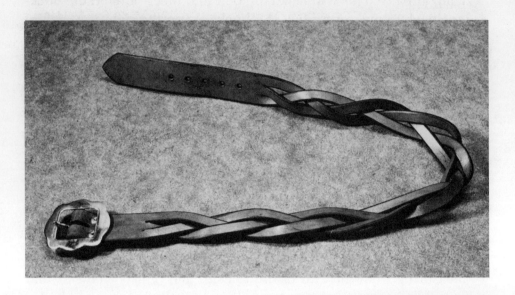

MATERIALS

buckle, with or without a tongue (when you buy your materials, choose the buckle first so you can get the leather to fit)

strip of latigo or oak-tanned cowhide, about 8 oz., wide enough to fit the buckle and about 3½ to 4 feet long, depending on the waist measurement (see step 1, below)

practice strap of the same or similar leather, 1½" wide and 12" long

Finish; dye, paint if desired

two rivets or ¼" Chicago posts

TOOLS

razor cutter

edger

#5 punch, #0 punch (optional), slot punch (optional)

for drive punch: mallet, anvil, rubber soling material

This braid looks impossible, because there's no end to it, so I call it Mystery Braid. You can put it on any strap—a belt, shoulder strap, wristband, or a decorative strap on any project. Get a strap to learn on, and practice the braid a few times before you do the belt. It's not hard to do—just hard to explain.

1. Measure the person who will wear the belt as in step 1, page 89. Add 9½ inches to the measurement instead of 7½, because the braid takes up a little of the length, especially if your braid is tight. If the belt turns out to be too long, you can always cut off the end. Cut the belt to length.
2. Cut the end in a point, as in step 3, page 89.
3. Decide how long you want the braided part of the belt to be. You can braid a short section in the middle of the belt, or braid most of the length, as in the picture.
4. Mark the slits for the braid. For your practice strap, start the slits about one inch from each end. For the belt with full-length braid, start the slits about 5 inches from the buckle end and 8 or 9 inches from the point end. Measure and mark the strap or belt into three strips of equal width. Make pencil dots in several places along the leather and connect them with two ruled lengthwise lines.

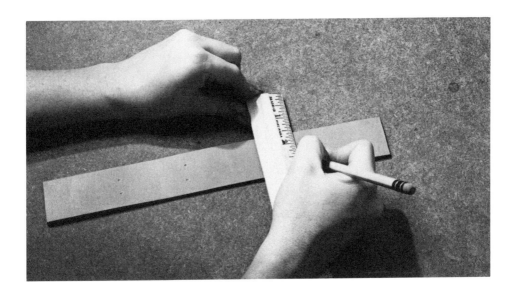

5. Before you cut, make sure your razor cutter has a good sharp blade. (I put in a new blade each time I cut braid slits.) Sink the blade in at one end of the pencil line, hold the blade straight up and down, and pull the leather with your other hand. Do not move the razor cutter at all. Pull slowly, and keep moving your pulling hand up closer to the cutter. Watch what you're doing, and you'll be able to cut exactly on the line. Cut the second slit the same way.

6. Punch a tiny hole (#0 punch) at each end of both slits. You don't have to do this, but it makes the slits easier to edge and nicer-looking.
7. Bevel all the edges, front and back. To edge up close to the end of a slit, put the strap on the edge of the table and hold it so that one of the small strips hangs off the edge.
8. If you want to use Acrylic Antique Finish, use it now. Put it on really thick so as to get Finish on all the edges, then wipe off the extra, as usual. Let the strap or belt dry for about half an hour.
9. Now, braid! Start from the end close to you (the lower end), and braid in the usual way: put left over middle, then right over middle. *Stop right there.* Hold onto the braided part with your left hand to keep it from untwisting.

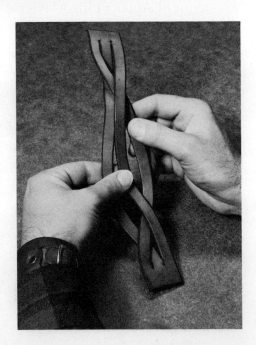

Now, at the other (upper) end of the strap, you'll see that the strip which begins at the left-hand corner passes between the other two. Put the upper end of the strap back through that same space and bring it around to the left, *keeping the front side facing you.* Don't let go of the braid with your left hand. At this point, your strap will look like a twisted mess; the middle strip will have a real corkscrew look (3). That's fine.

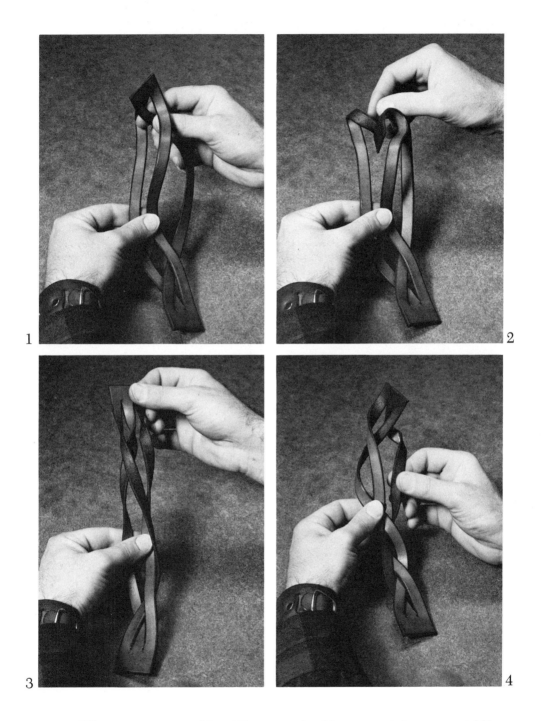

When you stopped braiding, you had just put right over middle.
So put left over middle, then right over middle, then left over
middle. *Stop again* (4).

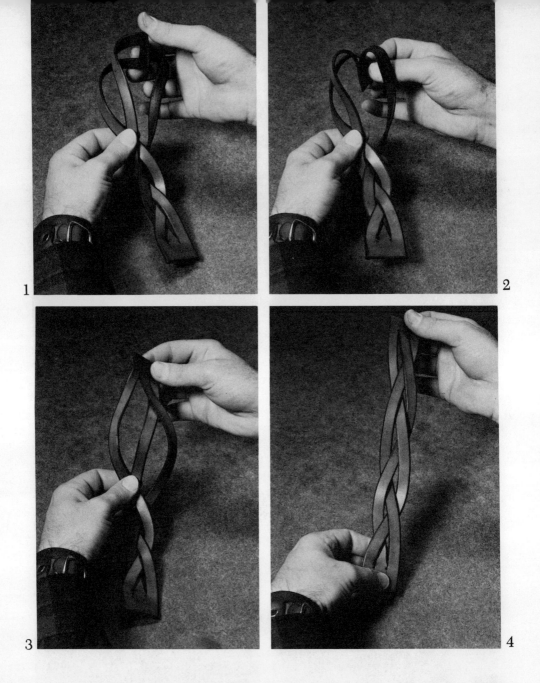

You are going to twist the top of the strap through again. Hold onto the braided part with your left hand, as before. Again, you'll see that the strip which begins at the left-hand corner passes between the other two. To see this more clearly, you can pull the top apart a bit (without letting go of the braid). Put the end of the strap through that same space and bring it around to the right, *keeping the front side facing you.*

For your practice strap, stop now; you have one cycle of braid. For the belt, repeat the process, putting right over middle and left over middle and then twisting the top end through, until the braid fills the belt strap. Each two times that you put the end through, you should come out with a flat braid.

10. Put the buckle on the belt and punch holes in the other end as for the plain belt (steps 7–8, pages 90-91).

Visor

MATERIALS

6–7 oz. yellow latigo (take pattern along when you go to buy leather)

Finish; dye, paint if desired

2 feet of ⅛″ calf or goat lacing

⅝″ buckle

one rivet

TOOLS

cutter

edger

#0 punch, #5 punch

⅝″ or ¾″ slot punch (optional)

for drive punch: mallet, rubber soling material

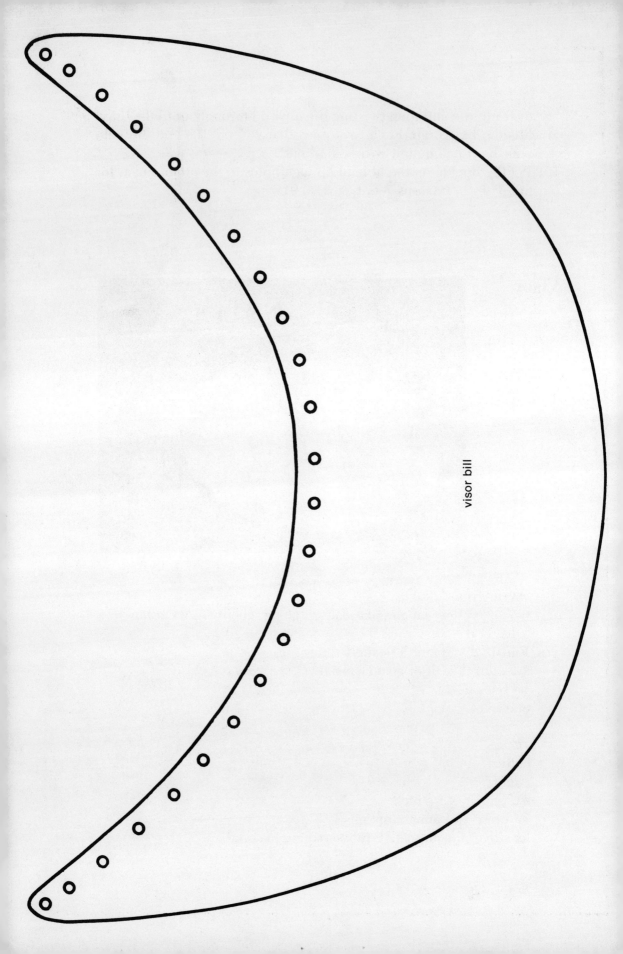

visor bill

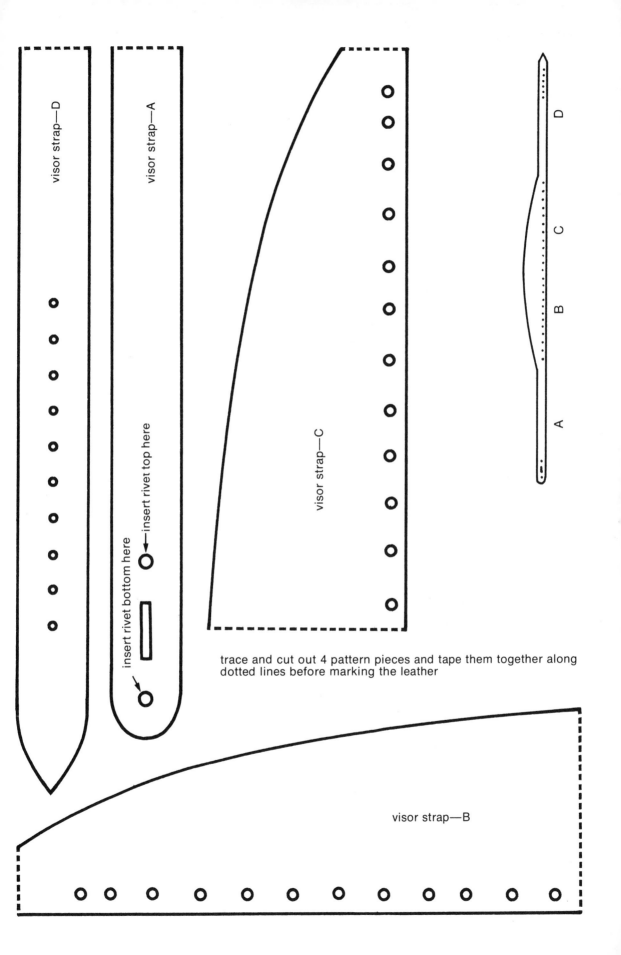

visor strap—D

visor strap—A

insert rivet top here

insert rivet bottom here

visor strap—C

trace and cut out 4 pattern pieces and tape them together along
dotted lines before marking the leather

D

C

B

A

visor strap—B

decorating tools (stamps, etc.)
for stamping: mallet, marble (optional)
lacing needle
metal hammer
anvil

1. Trace the pattern pieces, cut them out, and tape them together on the dotted lines.
2. Use a pencil to draw the pattern on the smooth side of the leather; mark the holes, too. Notice that there are only two leather pieces (bill and strap). If you have more than two, you forgot to tape the paper pattern pieces together; fix it before cutting the leather!
3. Cut out the leather pieces.
4. Bevel the edges, front and back.
5. Punch holes—#0 for lacing the pieces together, and #5 for the rivet. Punch the slot for the buckle tongue, as the pattern shows. If you don't have a slot punch, nibble a slot with the #5 punch. Don't worry if it isn't perfect; it won't show. On the other end of the strap, the holes for the buckle tongue can be either #0 or #5, depending on how big the buckle tongue is—try one out to see. If #5 is too big and #0 is too small, you can make one halfway in between by nibbling with the #0 punch.
6. Decorate as you wish. When you plan your design, note that the lacing holes are on the *lower* edge of the strap. Don't get it upside down!
7. Dye the pieces if you are going to, then use Acrylic Antique Finish. Last, use paint to color small areas. Give the pieces an hour or so to dry if you use paint, so the designs won't smear.
8. Place the bill piece over the strap piece and lace the strap and bill together. Use a running stitch (page 58). At the lace ends, you can lace backward for one stitch and tie the lace to itself. Put the visor on the anvil, and gently tap the lacing flat with the metal hammer.
9. Put in the buckle (check to make sure it goes in the right direction before you do the rivet—see photo on page 90) and then put in a rivet. Hold the buckle off the edge of the anvil, and pound the rivet flat with the metal hammer.
10. Buff up the visor, and it's done! It may seem stiff at first, but it will soon mold to fit your head; that's one of the nicest things about leather.

Dog Collar

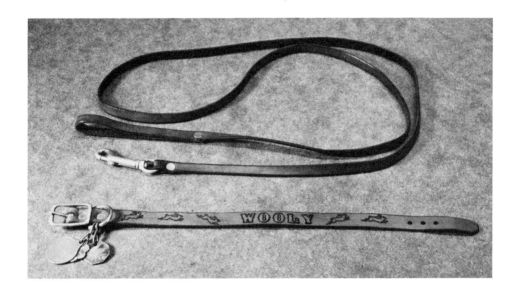

MATERIALS

6–7 oz. latigo or oak-tanned cowhide, a strip about 4″–5″
    longer than the neck measurement and whatever width
    looks right for your dog (¾″ is a good width for a dog that
    eats medium-sized Milkbones)
Finish; dye, paint if desired
buckle to match the leather width (solid brass is best)
D-ring to match the leather width (solid brass is best)—to
    hold tags
2 rivets, solid brass
neat's-foot oil or Lexol (optional, for later use)

TOOLS

cutter
edger
decorating tools (stamps, etc.)
for stamping: mallet, marble (optional)
#5 punch, slot punch (optional)
for drive punch: rubber soling material
metal hammer
anvil

1. Measure the dog's neck—not really tight, but just the way you want the collar to fit. Add about 4 inches for overlap and the buckle, perhaps a little more for a very big dog. Remember, you can always cut the collar off if it's too long. Cut the leather strip to length, and cut a point on the end of the strip, to make it go through the buckle more easily.
2. Bevel the edges, front and back.
3. Decorate the collar as you like. Remember to dampen the leather first if you are stamping on oak-tanned cowhide.
4. Use Acrylic Antique Finish, then paint if desired.
5. Punch a slot for the buckle tongue. Start the slot about 1½ inches from the unpointed end of the strip; the slot should be about ⅝ inch long. If you don't have a slot punch, you can nibble a slot with the #5 punch.
6. Put in the buckle, and check to make sure that it's going the right way. Then punch holes for a rivet to hold on the buckle. When you pound the rivet, hold the buckle off the side of the anvil so you won't hit the buckle with the hammer. Slip on the D-ring, with its flat side between the collar and the overlap, then put in another rivet to hold the D-ring in place. Again, hold the buckle and D-ring off the side of the anvil.
7. Buff up the collar when it's dry, and try it on the dog to see where to punch the holes for the buckle. Punch the holes, put the tags on the D-ring, and present the collar to its proud owner!
8. Dog collars and leashes usually get a lot of wear, in all kinds of weather, so put some oil on after a few weeks, to keep the leather from drying out and cracking. Neat's-foot oil or Lexol works fine. Repeat the application of oil every month or so.

Matching Leash

MATERIALS
6-9 oz. latigo or oak-tanned cowhide, strip 6 feet long or longer; width—again, whatever goes with your dog, also depending on the width of the leash clip you find. ¾" is a good width for a medium dog
Finish; dye, paint if desired

leash clip
2 rivets
neat's-foot oil or Lexol (optional, for later use)

TOOLS
cutter
edger
#5 punch
for drive punch: mallet, rubber soling material
decorating tools (stamps, etc.)
for stamping: mallet, marble (optional)
metal hammer
anvil

1. Decide how long you want the leash. Add about 6 inches for the handhold, and cut the strip to length.
2. Bevel the edges, front and back.
3. Decorate with stamps or whatever. Dampen oak-tanned first.
4. Apply Acrylic Antique Finish heavily, as usual, and wipe off the excess. When the Finish has dried for a few minutes (fifteen or so) you can paint the stamped places if you wish.
5. Wrap one end of the strap around the leash clip, punch holes, and put in a rivet.
6. At the other end, turn the strap back to make a place to hold onto the leash—about 6 inches is good—punch holes, and put in a rivet.
7. Polish up the leash with a shoe brush or a rag.

Belt Pouch

MATERIALS
6–7 oz. yellow latigo (take the pattern with you when you go
    to buy the leather)
Finish; dye, paint if desired
4 rivets
1″ brass ring
3/16″ latigo lacing, about a yard is plenty

TOOLS
cutter
edger
#5 punch
for drive punch: mallet, rubber soling material
decorating tools (stamps, etc.)
for stamping: mallet, marble (optional)
metal hammer
anvil
lacing needle

1. Trace the pattern, and cut it out.
   The shape of a belt pouch is one thing everyone seems to want a special way. If you want yours longer, narrower, wider, etc., you might want to try your hand at making your own pattern. You can see that the holes have to match up, and that the front and back pieces should be the same shape. Try folding the paper to get an even or symmetrical shape. When you think you have the size and shape you want, tape the pattern together to make sure it works and it's what you want. Also, instead of starting from scratch, you can start from this pattern and add or take away—why not try it?
2. Draw around the pattern onto the leather, using a pencil. Mark the holes, too.
3. Cut out the five leather pieces.
4. Bevel the edges, front and back.
5. Punch holes, for lacing and rivets. Cut the slit and punch the hole for the ring.

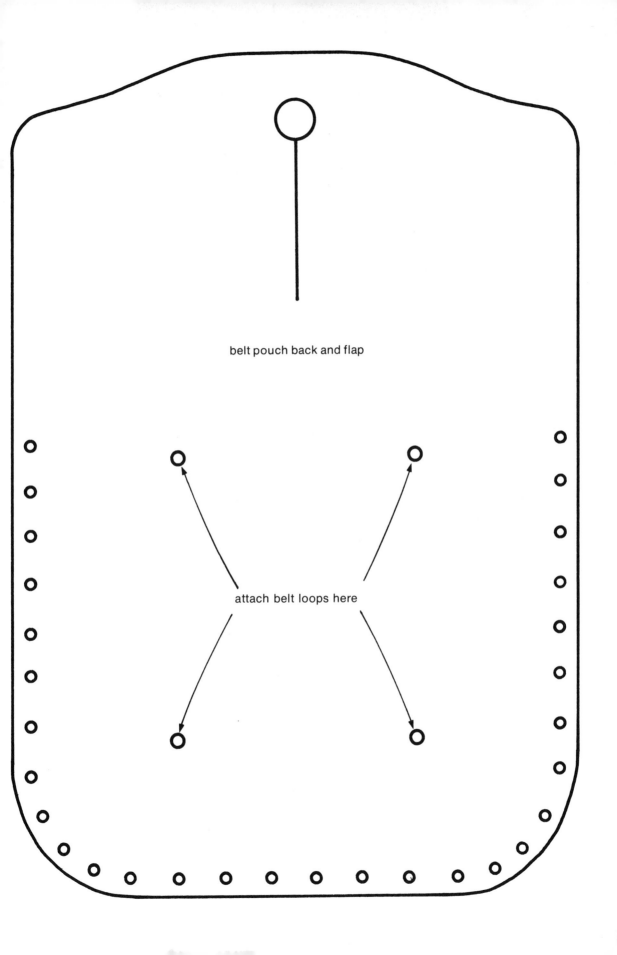

belt pouch back and flap

attach belt loops here

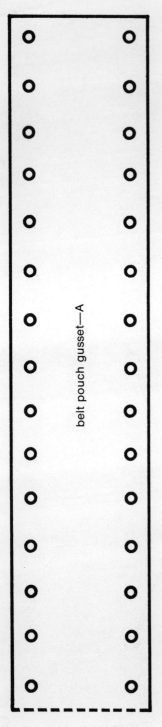

belt pouch gusset—A

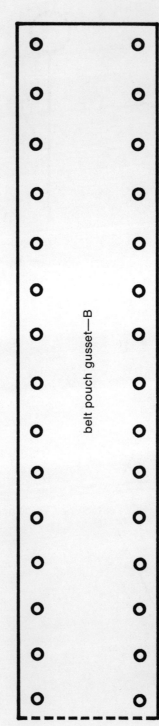

belt pouch gusset—B

belt loop (cut 2)

trace and cut out 2 pattern pieces and tape them together along dotted lines before marking the leather

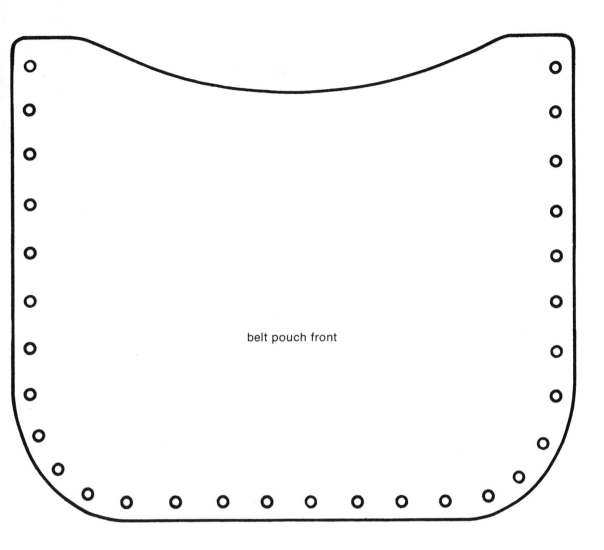

belt pouch front

6. Decorate as you wish—stamps, swivel knife, V-gouge . . .
7. Use dye, paint, and/or Acrylic Antique Finish. Finish the lacing, too.
8. Rivet the straps to the back/flap piece.
9. Tie a 6-inch piece of lacing to the ring. Put the lacing ends through the holes in the front piece, and tie the ends together on the inside in a square knot. Tap the knot flat with the hammer, on the anvil.
10. Lace the pieces together—lace the front to the gusset (side and bottom), then the back/flap to the gusset. Use a running stitch, with the gusset underneath the other piece, and tie a single knot at the lace ends.
11. Buff up the belt pouch.

Notebook Cover

MATERIALS

paper: get this part first so you'll know how much leather you need. You can use a whole spiral notebook, either removing the paper covers or leaving them on. In this case you will lace the leather cover to the spiral. Or you can use a stack of punched notebook paper; for this you'll need rings. Stationery, art supply, and dime stores have blank paper, notebooks, date/phone books, photo albums, diaries, etc. that you can use.

rings, if you'll be using them—get the kind that snap open and shut (also from stationery store)

lacing, if you're using a spiral notebook

4-9 oz. latigo or oak-tanned cowhide

TOOLS

cutter

edger

#5 drive punch, #0 punch (for calf lacing)

for drive punch: mallet, anvil, rubber soling material

decorating tools (stamps, etc.)

for stamping: mallet; anvil or marble

lacing needle (optional)

1. Make a pattern. Wrap a piece of paper around the notebook insides, to make sure the leather will be big enough (a). Allow a little extra, especially if the leather is thick. Remember, if you cut the leather too big, there's no problem—you can just trim it. But if you

cut it too small, there's nothing you can do, except go get a smaller notebook filler.

2. Draw around the pattern onto the leather, and cut out the leather.
3. Bevel the edges, front and back.
4. Mark hole placement for the rings or lacing. *For a spiral notebook:* Draw a light ruled pencil line down the middle of the leather piece, on the inside. Set the notebook next to the line, and make a dot on the line where each ring of the spiral touches the leather. Take away the notebook. Mark *two* rows of dots for holes, one on either side of the center line and about ¼ inch away, using the first dots you made as a guide to spacing the holes. *For rings:* Place the whole stack of paper on the leather where it will be when the notebook is finished. Fold the leather over the paper to make sure the placement is correct. Open the leather flat again—carefully, so as not to move the paper—and mark through each paper hole to the leather. Put the paper on the other half of the leather to mark holes in that half.
5. Punch holes for the rings or lacing (b). Hole size depends on the lacing: #0 for calf lacing, #5 for latigo.
6. Decorate the leather—stamps, carving . . .
7. Color the leather as you like, front and back. Dye the lacing at the same time, if it isn't dyed already. Let dry thoroughly.
8. Put the paper inside the leather cover. Dampen oak-tanned leather where the cover folds, to make it mold to shape. Put in the rings or

lacing. To lace a spiral notebook in, use a whipstitch: thread the lacing through the leather, around the spiral, and through the leather again. Tie the ends of the lacing to a stitch on the inside of the notebook cover.

Hatchet Cover

MATERIALS
5–7 oz. latigo or oak-tanned leather (take the pattern with you
   when you go to buy leather)
Finish, if desired
rubber cement
waxed nylon thread
brass snap
neat's-foot oil or Lexol for later use (optional)

TOOLS
cutter
edger
#0 punch, #5 punch

for drive punch: mallet, rubber soling material
decorating tools (stamps, etc.)
for stamping: mallet, marble (optional)
stitch marker (optional)
2 harness needles
snap setter
metal hammer
anvil

1. Make a pattern—follow the diagram. Draw around your hatchet. Leather takes up space when it's wrapped around something, and you need room for the stitching, so add ½ inch on the lower edge and on the cutting edge. Check the pattern by wrapping it around the hatchet and taping the paper together. It should fit loosely.
2. Draw around the paper pattern onto the leather, and cut out the piece.
3. Cut the slits for the belt to pass through, and punch #5 holes, one at each end of both slits. These holes help to spread out any strain on the slit, so it won't tear.
4. Bevel all the edges, front and back.
5. Stamp in designs, if you are going to. Dampen the leather first, if it's oak-tanned.
6. If desired, apply Acrylic Antique Finish thickly on front and back, and wipe off all the excess. Let the piece dry for about twenty minutes. (The hatchet cover in the photo was done without Acrylic Antique Finish.)

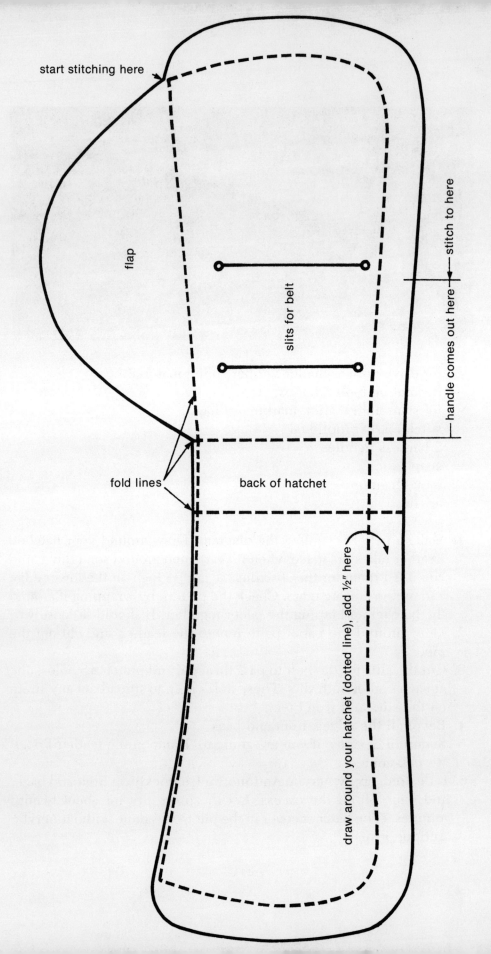

start stitching here

flap

stitch to here

slits for belt

handle comes out here

fold lines

back of hatchet

draw around your hatchet (dotted line), add ½" here

7. To line up the edges for the sewing holes, you can rubber cement them together. Apply rubber cement to both layers, wait twenty minutes, then stick them together. (Dampen the leather, if it is oak-tanned, to make it fold more easily.) Mark the hole spacing—about five holes to the inch—and punch.
8. Stitch the seam, using waxed nylon thread, harness needles, and a double running stitch (page 61). At the end, get both needles to the same side of the leather, and tie the threads in a square knot. Put the leather on the anvil, and gently tap the whole seam and the knot flat with the hammer.
9. Slip in the hatchet, and mark where the snap should go. Punch holes, and set the snap. Oak-tanned leather can be dampened again to make the hatchet cover conform well to the shape of the hatchet.
10. Buff up the hatchet cover—use neutral shoe cream wax if you like more shine than you get with the shoe brush by itself.
11. A hatchet cover usually gets a lot of outside wear, and it could use some oil every few weeks to keep the leather from drying out and cracking.

Chessboard or Checkerboard

MATERIALS
5–6 oz. oak-tanned cowhide or 6–7 oz. yellow latigo, piece at
    least 24″ square
dye, preferably a very dark color
⅝″ plywood, piece 22″ square
rubber cement
about 60 tacks—shoe tacks or upholstery tacks; any kind will
    do
felt or suede for the back side, piece 22″ square (optional)
Finish

TOOLS
cutter
V-gouge
decorating tools (stamps, etc.) if desired

for stamping: mallet; anvil or marble
metal hammer

1. Make a pattern. Use a large piece of paper and a T-square, or something to make good square corners with. First draw a perfect square, 16 inches on each side. Mark off the little squares with a ruler—eight squares on a side, each one 2 inches square. Draw the lines. Keep checking to make sure that all the squares come out the same. Then measure out from the 16-inch square, 3¾ inches on each side. This will give you a big square, with 3 inches all around the chessboard for a border, plus ¾ inch to fold around the plywood edges. Cut out the big square. It's better to plan the chessboard on paper like this, instead of directly on the leather, because any mistakes you might make when planning would show up at least a little.
2. Place the pattern on the leather, and hold it down firmly with heavy objects: books, shears, anvil, etc. Draw around the pattern with a pencil, and draw over the lines for the small squares, with the pattern still held in place. Just draw on top of the paper, using a ruler as a guide. If you press medium hard, the pencil will make a mark on the leather. You might take a careful look to check the markings. Take off the pattern and check the lines with the ruler.

114

3. Cut the leather square out (the big square).

4. Practice making V-gouge cuts on a scrap of the same leather. The cut should be deep enough to see clearly, but less than half the thickness of the leather, or the leather will be weakened. When you have the V-gouge adjusted and are familiar with the way it works, slowly make the cuts in the chessboard, along the lines for the small squares. If you like, you can also make other cuts in the border for decoration; if you do, draw the lines with the pencil first. Go slow, and keep the V-gouge flat on the leather.

5. Use stamps to make designs in the border, if desired. If you are using oak-tanned leather, dampen it before stamping. Make light pencil guidelines first, to keep the stamping even.

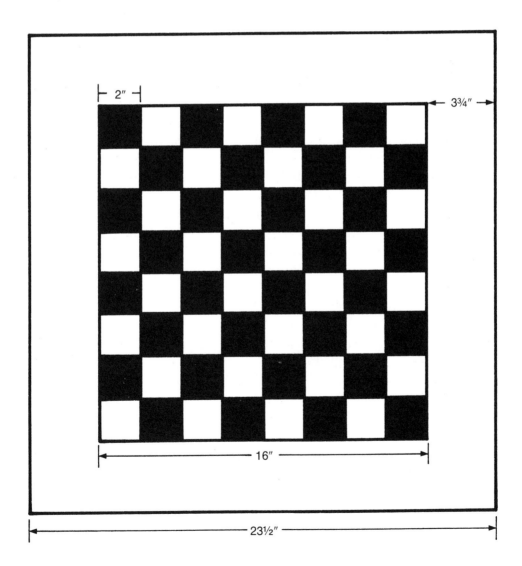

6. Dye every other square, as shown. Use leather dye (not paint, not Finish) and a small paintbrush. A very dark color will give the most contrast. To help in dyeing the squares without mistakes, pour a little of the dye into the cap of the bottle, and set the cap on a thick piece of cardboard near the square you want to dye. Then you won't be moving the brush over the whole chessboard each time you need more dye. The dye smells strong, and this step should be done in a well-ventilated area. You can set some cardboard squares on the squares you *don't* want to dye, to protect them from splashes, but don't use tape, because it marks the leather. Don't worry about getting dye into the V-gouge lines; the Finish will darken them anyway. To get a dark color, go over the dyed squares at least twice with the dye. Let the dye dry several hours— overnight is best.

7. Measure and cut a ¾-inch square out of each corner of the leather. This is to let the leather fold around the wood.

8. Turn the leather upside down on a smooth surface, and put the plywood piece on it. The corners of the plywood piece should be right at the corners of the little cutout squares. Draw around the plywood onto the leather, to mark where the leather will fold. Take away the wood, and make V-gouge cuts along the lines, on the *back* side of the leather—to help the leather fold smoothly around the wood.

9. Apply rubber cement to the wood, top and sides, and to the back side of the leather. Make the glue coat even and fairly heavy, and make sure it goes all the way to the edges. Let the glue dry until it is no longer wet—about twenty minutes—setting it in the sun helps. Then lay the leather face down on a smooth surface, and press the wood in place, carefully.

   Turn the chessboard right side up, and dampen the edges (on the top side of the leather) so that they will mold around the wood. A sponge works well for this. Press the edges to the wood with your hands, then stand the chessboard on edge and tap the sides flat to the wood with the hammer. Make sure the surface of your hammer is smooth, and then tap gently all over the chessboard to flatten it and make the glue stick. If there are any little bits of glue on the top side of the leather, let them dry, and rub them off with your fingers.

10. Dampen the surface and edges of the chessboard evenly, if you are

using oak-tanned leather. Apply Acrylic Antique Finish *thickly* to the entire surface and edges, all at once. Don't rub the finish in, just smear it all over. Then wipe off all the excess, right away, using paper towels and a light circular motion, to avoid streaks. If the surface is not evenly colored, put on Neutral (no color) Acrylic Antique Finish *thickly,* and wipe it off. Let the chessboard dry for an hour or so.

11. Stand the chessboard on edge, and pound in tacks around the edges—perhaps one tack every 2 inches.

12. If you like, cut out a 22-inch square piece of felt, soft leather, or suede, and glue it to the back of the chessboard.

13. When the Acrylic Antique Finish has dried overnight, you can use a neutral shoe cream (wax) and a shoe brush to buff up the chessboard. Or for a little less shine, just use the shoe brush.

You can make other game boards in the same way—Parchesi, for example.

Knapsack

MATERIALS

leather: oak-tanned is probably too stiff, but almost any other kind of leather will do, depending on whether you prefer a soft or stiff knapsack, how lightweight you want it to be, etc. Heavy chrome-tanned (about 4–5 oz.) or lightweight latigo (about 4–5 oz.) would work well. Take the pattern with you when you go to buy the leather

2 shoulder straps about 1½" wide and about 18" long, the same finish leather as the main piece or a little heavier; chrome-tanned or latigo

Finish

about 8 feet of lacing or heavy waxed nylon thread, whichever you would like to use, for the side seams

2 snaps to hold flap shut

8 rivets for attaching straps

TOOLS
cutter
edger
#5 drive punch, #0 punch if you are sewing
for drive punch: mallet, rubber soling material
lacing needle (if you are going to lace the seams) or harness
    needle (if you are going to sew the seams with thread)
metal hammer
anvil
snap setter

1. Make the pattern—it's a rectangle, 12 inches wide and 25½ inches long. Cut out the corners to make the flap as shown, 1½ inches down and 2½ inches in on each side. Fold the paper pattern up so that it looks like the knapsack—letting about 1½ inches fold over for

the flap—and see if it's the size and shape you want. Change it if not.

2. Draw the pattern onto the leather, holding the pattern in place with something heavy. Cut out the leather piece.

3. Bevel the edges, if the leather is heavy enough. Bevel the shoulder strap edges, front and back.

4. If you are using lightweight latigo, you can put Acrylic Antique Finish on the piece now. Use Finish on the shoulder straps.

5. Punch holes for lacing or sewing the side seams. For lacing, the #5 holes should be about ¼ inch from the edge, and ½ inch apart, or closer. For sewing, the #0 holes should be very close together— about four holes to the inch, and about ⅛ inch from the edge. Mark the holes on the front part down to the fold line. Punch these holes, then mark through them to the back piece, and punch those holes. If you try to punch both layers at once, the pieces will slip around.

6. Fold the piece so that it is *wrong side out,* and sew or lace the side

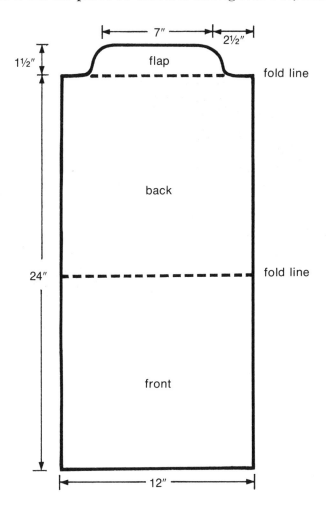

seams. You can use any kind of stitch you want—running stitch, whipstitch, double running stitch, even cross stitch. Make the thread or lacing tight, for strength.

7. Turn the bag right side out. To make the sides lie flat, put the bag on the anvil and gently tap the sewing or lacing flat with the metal hammer.

8. Put some things in the bag, just as you will when using it, and mark where you want the snaps to hold the flap shut. Punch #5 holes, and set the snaps.

9. Have someone help you mark where you want the shoulder straps to be attached to the bag and how long you want them. 18 inches should fit most people. Punch holes in the bag and the shoulder strap ends, and rivet on the straps. To punch a hole in the bag, you'll have to use a drive punch. Put the anvil and rubber soling piece inside the bag, so they'll be under the place where you want to punch. When you set the rivets, place the anvil inside the bag, under the rivets.

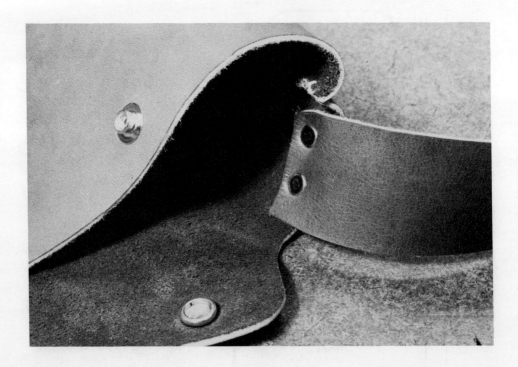

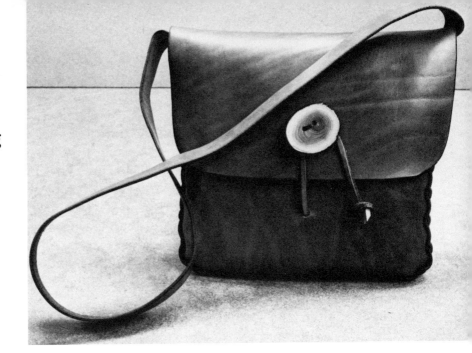

Shoulder Strap Bag

MATERIALS

6–7 oz. yellow latigo (take the pattern with you when you go
 to buy the leather)

shoulder strap to match, about 3 feet long, 1½" wide

Finish; dye, paint if desired

a button (at least 1" in diameter) for the front—could be
 wood, bone, brass, leather—this is up to you; button
 should have large holes (see step 8)

3/16" latigo lacing to match leather, about 7 feet long

TOOLS

cutter

edger

#5 punch, #0 punch (optional)

for drive punch: mallet, rubber soling material

decorating tools (stamps, etc.)

for stamping: mallet, marble (optional)

lacing needle

metal hammer

anvil

1. Make the pattern. To make a shape that is the same on both sides,
 fold the paper in half to draw the curve. To make the front piece
 the same curve as the back and flap, make one first and draw

121

around it to make the other. You can change the measurements to whatever you like, as long as the front and back match, so that they can be laced together. Also, the flap can be any shape you choose.

Mark holes in the pattern, for lacing. The middle of each hole should be ¼ inch from the edge of the pattern. The holes should be about ½ inch apart, from the middle of one hole to the middle of the next hole. Mark the holes on one of the pattern pieces, then punch holes in that pattern piece and use it to mark the other pattern piece. This is to make sure that the holes line up.

2. Hold the pattern in place with something heavy and draw around the pattern onto the leather.
3. Cut out the leather pieces. Also cut out a shoulder strap about 3 feet long and 1½ inches wide. Make slits in the ends of the shoulder strap, dividing the strap in two, for about 2 inches.
4. Bevel all the edges, including the slits in the strap.
5. Punch the holes. Punch #0 holes at the ends of the slits on the strap for a nicer finish.
6. Decorate as you wish, with stamps, swivel knife, holes, etc.
7. Color the leather pieces, including the lacing.
8. When the purse pieces have dried for about fifteen minutes, put the button on the flap. Punch two holes in the flap where you want the button, and lace the button on. Tie a square knot in the lacing ends, on the inside of the flap. Leave the button a tiny bit loose, so

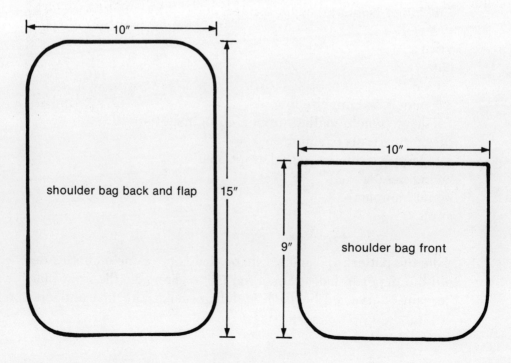

there will be room for the lacing, which will wrap around it. If you can't get lacing through the holes on the button, you could use heavy waxed nylon thread instead.

Punch a hole near the bottom of the front piece, and put in the piece of lacing that will wrap around the button. Tie a single knot on the inside of the front piece, to hold it there. And tie a single knot at the end of the lace, to make it look good and be easy to use.

9. Lace the front and back/flap pieces together. Use a lacing needle and a running stitch, page 58. Tie a single knot in the end of the lacing. Put the back/flap over the front piece, and lace in and out and in and out . . . It may not look like it will work, but it will! Pull the lacing snug as you go. Tie a square knot in the lacing ends, and tap on the knot with the hammer, on an anvil, to flatten the knot.

10. Punch holes and rivet the shoulder strap onto the bag.

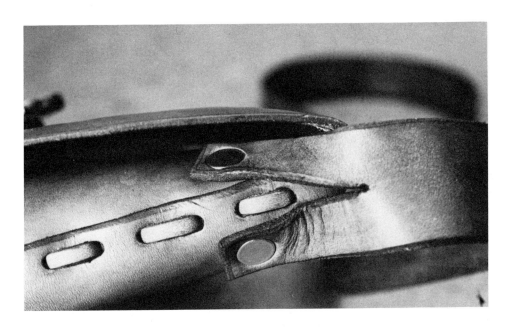

11. Buff up the bag with a shoe brush or a rag, and some neutral shoe cream if you like a really glossy look.

The bag will probably seem a bit stiff at first, but it will soften and shape to a rounder look as you use it.

Scraps

When you've made a few things out of leather, you'll notice a growing pile of scraps—good leather, but strange shapes and sizes. There are *many* things you can do with scraps. You can make regular projects out of them, by piecing them together—sewing, lacing, or riveting. Here are a few other ideas:

collage	door plaque
earrings	dried flower holder
ring	gingerbread person, Christmas tree ornament
earmuffs	leather "beads"
puzzle	handles, drawer pulls, hinges

Suppliers

	SELL BY MAIL ORDER?	LEATHER IN SMALL QUANTITIES?	STRIPS FOR BELTS, ETC.?	ACRYLIC ANTIQUE FINISH?	TOOLS?	PATTERNS FOR PROJECTS?	CATALOG?
Berman Leathercraft 147 South Street Boston, Mass. 02111	yes	yes	yes	yes	yes	no	yes
Century Leather Co., Inc. 110 Beach Street Boston, Mass. 02111	yes	yes	yes	yes	yes	yes	yes
Cleveland Leather Co. 2824 Lorain Avenue Cleveland, Ohio 44113	yes	yes	yes	yes	yes	yes	yes
Colo-Craft 1310 S. Broadway Denver, Colo. 80210	yes	no	yes	yes	yes	yes	yes
The Dead Cow 1040 River Street Santa Cruz, Calif. 95060	yes	yes	yes	yes	yes	yes	no
D'Narb Ltd. 100 Myrtle Avenue Havertown, Pa. 19083	yes	yes	yes	yes	yes	no	yes
Double D Leather Co. 6212 D Madison Pike Huntsville, Ala. 35806	yes	yes	yes	yes	yes	yes	yes
Drake Leather Co., Inc. 3500 W. Beverly Blvd. Montebello, Calif. 90640	yes	yes	yes	yes	yes	yes	yes
Funk and Rose 212 S. 15th Avenue Minneapolis, Minn. 55404	yes	yes	yes	no	yes	no	yes

	SELL BY MAIL ORDER?	LEATHER IN SMALL QUANTITIES?	STRIPS FOR BELTS, ETC.?	ACRYLIC ANTIQUE FINISH?	TOOLS?	PATTERNS FOR PROJECTS?	CATALOG?
Leather 19 E. Woodside Avenue Ardmore, Pa. 19003	yes	yes	yes	yes	yes	no	no
Leather, Etc. 2033 University Avenue Berkeley, Calif. 94704	yes	yes	yes	yes	yes	yes	no
Leather Unlimited Co. P. O. Box 23002 Milwaukee, Wis. 53223	yes	yes	yes	no	yes	yes	yes
The Leather Works 628 Emerson Street Palo Alto, California 94301	yes	yes	yes	yes	yes	yes	yes
Leathercrafters' Supply Co. 25 Great Jones (E. 3rd) Street New York, N.Y. 10012	yes	yes	yes	yes	yes	yes	yes
Leon Leather Co., Inc. 1738 East 2nd Street Scotch Plains, N.J. 07076	yes	yes	yes	yes	yes	yes	yes
Mac Leather Co. 424 Broome Street New York, N.Y. 10013	yes	yes	yes	yes	yes	no	yes
Natural Leather 203 Bleecker Street New York, N.Y. 10012	yes	no	yes	no	yes	no	yes
New Haven Leather Co., Inc. 254 State Street New Haven, Conn. 06510	*yes	no	yes	yes	yes	no	no

*(in Conn. area)

	SELL BY MAIL ORDER?	LEATHER IN SMALL QUANTITIES?	STRIPS FOR BELTS, ETC.?	ACRYLIC ANTIQUE FINISH?	TOOLS?	PATTERNS FOR PROJECTS?	CATALOG?
J. G. Read & Bros. Co., Inc. 101 21st Street, Box 469 Ogden, Utah 84402	yes	no	yes	yes	yes	yes	yes
Richmond Leather Co. 1839 West Broad Street Richmond, Virginia 23220	yes	yes	yes	yes	yes	yes	yes
S-T Leather Co. 329-33 E. Long Street Columbus, Ohio 43215 and 4018 Olive Street St. Louis, Mo. 63108	yes	no	yes	no	yes	no	yes
Southwestern Leather & Shoe Findings Co. 27 N. 3rd Avenue, Box 3555 Phoenix, Ariz. 85030	yes	yes	yes	no	yes	no	no
Worth Leather Co. 151 Allen Blvd. Farmingdale, N.Y. 11735	yes	yes	yes	yes	yes	no	yes
Tandy Leather Co. Many stores (look in the phone book)	yes	kits	yes	no	yes	yes	yes

1-800
433-5546

Suggestions for Further Reading

BRAIDING AND LACING

Faulkner, Jan. *Leathercraft by Hand*. New York: Walker & Co., 1973.
Grant, Bruce. *Leather Braiding*. Cambridge, Md.: Cornell Maritime Press, 1961.
How to Lace. New York: Drake Publishers, 1947.

CARVING

Cherry, Raymond. *General Leathercraft*. Bloomington, Ill.: McKnight & McKnight Publishing Co., 1955.
Stohlman, Al. *How to Carve Leather*. Craftool, 1952.
Stohlman, Al. *Inverted Leather Carving*. Craftool, 1961.
Stohlman, Al. *Tech Tips*. Craftool, 1969.

DOVER BOOKS FOR DESIGN IDEAS
(The following books are published by Dover Publications, New York, N.Y.)

African Designs from Traditional Sources by Geoffrey Williams, 1971.
The Book of Signs by Rudolf Koch, 1955.
Chinese Folk Designs by W. M. Hawley, 1949.
Decorative Art of the Southwestern Indians by Dorothy Smith Sides, 1961.
Design Motifs of Ancient Mexico by Jorge Encisco, 1947.
Greek Ornament, edited by Patrick Connell, 1968.
Hornung's Handbook of Designs and Devices by Clarence P. Hornung, 1946.
A Treasury of Design for Artists and Craftsmen by Gregory Mirow, 1969.
Victorian Stencils for Design and Decoration, selected by Edmund V. Gillon, Jr., 1968.